T0247668

BREAK THE WALL

Break the Wall offers a clear, concise guide to successfully leading digital transformation. Importantly, this is as much about culture and organizational empowerment as it is technology and business strategy. The authors have studied a wide range of companies who have been through this journey and distilled their collective experience and wisdom into seven key insights that will give you a tremendous advantage in yours.

—*Scott Brinker, VP Platform Ecosystem at HubSpot, Editor of chiefmartec.com*

"Digital Transformation" is probably one of the most popular business buzzwords these days, but the urgency of it is still real. At this point, most business leaders have a good sense of the "what" and the "why," especially because we see it every day in the leading brands who are capturing more of our spend. But the "how" can feel daunting. In "Break the Wall," the AMA does a masterful job of laying out why transformation is not just proclamations from the top and moving budgets around. It stems from a customer-first, data-first approach to looking at one's strategy. And when you do, it quickly becomes clear that removing the "walls" within most organizations, which were set up for an older vision of efficiency and control, becomes one of the most important accelerators of change. Whether it is linking data, bringing cross-functional teams together to improve customer journeys, speeding up time to market, or just bringing more diverse views together to drive innovation, breaking the walls must be a critical priority for the business -- beyond getting the tools, hiring the data scientists, and enhancing one's design skills. But that's not easy. The AMA's book does a masterful job of providing practical examples -- from large, small, B2C, B2B, and businesses across sectors -- that can provide guideposts for how to think through one's own roadmap for change. Every leadership team realizing that their change efforts have stalled, or who are even just beginning, need to read this book, share their learning, and use that to pinpoint the walls to break and the techniques for doing so.

—*David Edelman, Former CMO of Aetna & CVS*

Every major company is going through digital transformation, yet most of these efforts lead to limited success. In their book Break the Wall, the authors provide a clear roadmap for successful digital transformation. Anyone engaged in this journey should read this book.

—*Sunil Gupta, Edward W. Carter Professor of*
Business Administration at Harvard Business School

A rare work assembling the world's leading academics, professionals and thought leaders in confronting one of the great organizational challenges of today: how do we do anything with all of this data? Finally we have a title that can make the process of digital transformation real.

—*Neil Hoyne, Chief Measurement Strategist at Google*

Finally, a book about digital transformation that provides a roadmap to overcome organizational obstacles and achieve the goals that so many companies aspire to. Break the Wall breaks the mold, with provocative insights by its all-star authors with a narrative that is so clear and compelling that leadership teams across the enterprise will be inspired to embrace and act upon.

—*Ed Keller, CEO, The Keller Advisory Group*

The book offers an insightful and timely guidance for achieving digital transformation in a post-Covid highly competitive market. The authors managed to create an encompassing framework that emphasizes the iterative-adaptation process that is critical to achieving organizational change in a fast-paced environment. Each chapter provides actionable nuggets, making the book a mirror for executives seeking to identify why existing efforts may not be as effective as expected.

—*Chris Leong, CMO, Schneider Electric*

Packed with pitfalls, stories, and straight talk perspectives from those on digital transformation journey, "Break the Wall: Why and How to Democratize Digital in your Business" is a fantastic handbook for today's leaders. The real-world insights, from different industries, gives all of us the path to close the gap between the current and desired status of our own digital transformation and build long-term organizational resiliency.

—*Diana O'Brien, Former CMO of Deloitte*

Definitely both a "why" and "how" book! Whether you're just now considering a digital transformation or already halfway through one, Break the Wall will give you cause for pause, along with the insights you'll need to ask the most useful questions, going forward.

—*Don Peppers, author, speaker, and customer experience authority*

AMA Leadership Series

BREAK THE WALL

Why and How to Democratize
Digital in Your Business

BY

ZEYNEP AKSEHIRLI

Northeastern University, USA

YAKOV BART

Northeastern University, USA

KWONG CHAN

Northeastern University, USA

AND

KOEN PAUWELS

Northeastern University, USA

United Kingdom – North America – Japan – India
Malaysia – China

Emerald Publishing Limited
Howard House, Wagon Lane, Bingley BD16 1WA, UK

First edition 2023

British Library Cataloguing in Publication Data
A catalogue record for this book is available from the British Library

ISBN: 978-1-80382-188-7 (Print)
ISBN: 978-1-80382-185-6 (Online)
ISBN: 978-1-80382-187-0 (Epub)

ISOQAR certified
Management System,
awarded to Emerald
for adherence to
Environmental
standard
ISO 14001:2004.

Certificate Number 1985
ISO 14001

INVESTOR IN PEOPLE

CONTENTS

AMA INTRODUCTION TO BOOK SERIES

Welcome to marketing in the twenty-first century – the age of data, social, mobile, automation, and globalization. The field is changing so quickly, it's difficult to keep up. There is an increasing uncertainty about the profession's mission and responsibilities. Meanwhile, the demands marketers face are ever more complex and critical.

This is why the American Marketing Association (AMA) has engaged some of the world's most innovative professionals, academics, and thought leaders to create The Seven Problems of Marketing – a seven-book series that introduces and explores a new set of organizing and actionable principles for the twenty-first-century marketer.

Each book in the series takes a deep dive into one problem, offering expertise, direction, and case studies while striking a balance between theory and application. The goal is to provide a contemporary framework for marketers as they navigate the unique challenges and vast opportunities of today's dynamic global marketplace.

Here are the seven problems addressed in the series:

Problem 1: Effectively targeting high-value sources of growth.

Problem 2: Defining the role of marketing in the firm and C-suite.

Problem 3: Managing the digital transformation of the modern corporation.

Problem 4: Generating and using insight to shape marketing practice.

Problem 5: Dealing with an omni-channel world.

Problem 6: Competing in dynamic, global markets.

Problem 7: Balancing incremental and radical innovation.

Importantly, the books in this series are written by and for marketers and marketing scholars. All of the conceptual and analytical frameworks offered are born from practice. The authors have applied their tools and methods in client settings, allowing them to test and refine their ideas in the face of real-world challenges. You'll read true stories about how marketers have used innovative thinking and practices to overcome seemingly impossible dilemmas and bring about game-changing success. Theories are explored in a way that busy marketers can understand viscerally. Client stories have been incorporated to illustrate how to apply the analysis frames as well as deal with application and practice-based issues.

Our fundamental aim with this series is to hone the practice of marketing for the twenty-first century. The AMA has asserted that there is a critical tension within every enterprise between "best" and "next" practices. Marketers often choose best practices because they are safe and proven. Next practices, which push boundaries and challenge conventions, can be riskier. Few enterprises, however, transform themselves and achieve breakout performance with best practices alone. The next practices discussed in this series are often responsible for driving outperformance. The books in this series are designed to engage you on two levels: individually, by increasing your knowledge and "bench strength," and organizationally, by improving the application of marketing concepts within your firm. When you finish each book, we are confident you will feel energized and think differently about the field of marketing and its organizing principles. Through the explanation of theory and compelling examples of its application, you will be empowered to help your organization quickly identify and maximize opportunities. After all, the opportunity to innovate and make an impact is what attracted most of us to the field of marketing in the first place.

Russ Klein
CEO, American Marketing Association

BOOK SERIES OVERVIEW

In 2016, the AMA established its first-ever intellectual agenda. This intellectual agenda focused on complex, challenging, and difficult-to-solve problems that would be of interest to both academics and practitioners. A working team of scholars and practitioners, selected by AMA leadership, identified seven big problems of marketing as the foundation of the agenda. These problems were ranked from a much longer list of challenges. These seven big problems shared three attributes: they were pressing issues that confronted every organization, they were C-suite level in scope, and they could not be solved by one article or book. Indeed, the team felt that each problem could trigger a decade-long research agenda. A key purpose of the AMA intellectual agenda was thus to stimulate research, dialogue, and debate among the entire AMA membership.

The purpose of the AMA book series is to shed a deeper light on each of the seven problems. In particular, the aim of the series is to enable readers to think differently and take action with regard to these big problems. Thus, the book series operates at two levels: individually, increasing your knowledge and bench strength, and at the organization level, improving the application of marketing concepts within your firm.

Given the nature of these problems, no single book or article can fully address the problem. By their very nature, these problems are significant, nuanced, and approachable from multiple vantage points. As such, each of the books provides a single perspective on the issue. This single perspective is intended to both advance knowledge and spark debate. While the books may emerge from academic literature and/or managerial application, their fundamental aim is to improve the practice of marketing. Books selected for the series are evaluated on six criteria:

1. *Seven Big Problems Focus*: Each book is focused on one of the seven big problems of marketing. These problems identify key conceptual issues in the field of marketing that are the focus of emerging academic research and that practitioners are actively confronting today.

2. *Audience*: The book is written primarily for an audience of thoughtful practitioners. Thoughtful in this context means that the practitioner is an active reader of both professional articles and books, is dedicated to enhancing his/her marketing knowledge and skills, and is committed to upgrading the organization's marketing culture, capabilities, and results. A secondary audience is academics (and students) and consultants.

3. *Integrated Framework*: The book provides an integrated framework that delineates the problem and offers a detailed approach for addressing it.

4. *Field-based Approach*: The authors have applied their frameworks in client settings. These client settings enable authors to test and refine their frameworks. Conceptual and analysis frameworks are enlivened via practice and case examples that demonstrate application in the field. Named and/or disguised client stories illustrate how to apply the analysis frames, how to deal with application issues, and other practice-based issues.

5. *Academic Literature*: The integrative frameworks should be new to the marketplace. The conceptual frameworks should extend existing thinking and the analysis frameworks should provide new ways to conduct marketing-related analysis.

6. *Readability*: The book should be intelligible to the average reader. The concepts should be clearly defined and explained, and cases written so that a reader can understand the content on a first read.

On behalf of the AMA, I am excited to bring these books to market. I am anxious to hear your feedback – both positive and challenging – as we move the field forward.

Bernie Jaworski
AMA Book Series Editor

BIOGRAPHY

Zeynep Aksehirli is an Associate Professor of Management and Organizational Development. Her academic interests lie at the intersection of various topics including organizational design, leadership, market strategy, and virtual work. She has published various articles and books on corporate culture, network structures, leadership competencies, and intranet design. Prior to joining Northeastern University, she taught at Boston College and NEU College of Professional Studies. Earlier, she was an Assistant Professor and Founding Faculty in Ozyegin University School of Business and Tuck School of Business in Dartmouth.

Yakov Bart is an Associate Professor of Marketing and Walsh Research Professor at Northeastern University. His research examining marketing implications of new digital technologies and business models has been funded with multiple research awards and grants. He presented at numerous academic conferences across the globe, and published in leading marketing and management journals, including *Marketing Science, Journal of Marketing Research, Journal of Marketing, Management Science*, and *Harvard Business Review*. His research published in *Decision Analysis* and *Journal of Interactive Marketing* won Best Paper awards. He has received several awards for outstanding teaching in Executive Education programs at INSEAD and teaching excellence at Northeastern University, and was named as one of the world's top 40 undergraduate business school professors by Poets&Quants. He is a frequent speaker at international business summits and industry events, including Teradata Analytics Universe and World Knowledge Forum.

Kwong Chan is an Academic Specialist at Northeastern University and serves as the Executive Director of the Digital, Analytics, Technology, and Automation Initiative at Northeastern University and Managing Director of the quantitative consulting firm Better Data

Group LLC. He leads teams to tackle challenges in the area of deep analytics and human behavior and has published research across domains including product innovation, advertising, public policy, engineering, and marketing.

Koen Pauwels is a distinguished Professor at Northeastern University and Co-director of its Digital, Analytics, Technology, and Automation (DATA) Initiative. He received his Ph.D. from UCLA, where he was chosen as a Top 100 Inspirational Alumnus. After getting tenure at Tuck, he helped build the startup Ozyegin University in Istanbul. Named a worldwide top 2% scientist, he has published 4 books and over 80 articles on marketing effectiveness that have received multiple awards from managers (Google, WPP, and Syntec), academics (O'Dell, Davidson, and Varadarajan) and institutions (Marketing Edge award for most promising research and the Gary Lilien Practice Prize). While writing this book, he was the President of the American Marketing Association's Academic Council.

PREFACE

Over the past 10 years, all Fortune 500 firms have undergone some form of digital transformation. This could be narrow transformation focused on migration from multi-channel to omni-channel marketing communication or a very broad transformation of the entire strategy of the firm. Somewhat surprisingly, it often the case that firms have taken a very narrow view – examining social media, big data, and the transformation of marketing communications. However, for those firms who recognize the tidal wave of digital change, the C-suite is focused on much larger issues of business model change, the reconfiguration of their value chain, and, in many cases the future competitive advantage of the firm. Certainly, this is very evident in the world of banking, platform firms such as Google, and in the hotly contested media and entertainment markets. However, even traditional industrial firms such Becton-Dickinson, Eastman Chemicals, Suffolk Construction, and Texas Instruments have taken a lead in transforming their sectors of the economy.

CEO driven transformation can be highly successful (e.g., Res-Med) or marked by very public failure (e.g., GE's Predix transformation). Fortunately, with the publication of *Break the Wall* – we now have a conceptual framework and specific practice-based recommendations to drive fundamental reinvention. A key insight – of authors Zeynep Aksehirli, Yakov Bart, Kwong Chan, and Koen Pauwels – is that there are multiple levels of transformation that progress at different paces – some parts of the organization support the change (IT unit) while others such as business units drive the innovation through experimentation to test the future. Their nested adaptive framework deploys a biology metaphor to explore several stages of transformation including initiation, implementation, resilience, and finally renewal of the business model. The main point is that the firm is constantly testing and adapting to the future. Drucker would term the challenge as managing "continuity and change" – so, firms can compete in both the present and in the future.

Importantly, like other volumes in the seven big problems series, this book is based on deep immersion with practice. The authors began their journey by depth interviews with leading practioners at various stages of their digital journeys. From this effort, seven key findings emerged. These findings, in turn, informed the development of their nested adaptive framework as well as the structure of the chapters in this volume. Hence, the beauty of this work is that it is from the ground-up, based on interviews, observations, and consulting combined with the best academic research on the subject.

As series Editor, I am very excited to share this cutting-edge, practice-based volume. It is both a catalyst for future research and a guidepost for leaders looking to drive or renew their digital transformation.

Bernie Jaworski

1

INTRODUCTION TO SEVEN KEY INSIGHTS

Late one afternoon in New York, we listened to a Chief Executive Officer (CEO) complain about the lack of progress in his company's digital transformation. "I don't get it" he sighs,

> we spend years getting all our data together in a lake and hiring the best data scientists to analyze it. Despite millions invested, I just don't see any impact on our business. What can I do?

"Well", we answered politely, "we just spent the day in your beautiful skyscraper building and noticed the data scientists all live on one floor and don't even have lunch at the same place as the managers. Talking to each, we noticed decision makers and data scientists had little interaction, yet plenty of stereotypes about each other. How do you expect the data science to influence the decision makers, and vice versa, if you have yet to manage the human factor? We recommended ensuring close cooperation between the business units demanding, and the data scientists delivering the digital goods." A year later, we were happy to see middle management and data scientists engaging closely in fast feedback cycles, answering business questions and improving tactics for the company's customers. Unfortunately, they were less happy with top management and information systems, as they perceived a lack of strategic support. "Where is the strategic vision?," "What are our swimming lanes?" and "How is leadership ensuring the whole organization and each of our careers improves with data-driven decision making?" are some of the comments we heard. High time to get back to the CEO to advise him anew.

As these experiences show, digital transformation is not easy, and means different things to different people and at different levels in the organization. Even the academic literature lacks a common definition, with most focusing on shiny new technologies.[1] However, digital transformation is an *organizational* transformation that changes how an organization *employs digital technologies*.[2] Indeed, a key observation we saw across industries and continents is that *the entire organization is changing, not just the interfaces with customers.* Structures, processes, workflow and decision rights are being transformed by digitization. Digital and social can be leveraged to generate new insights about employees and customers but more importantly to give them the tools to connect with each other and further the organization's goals. Done right, digital transformation not only enriches customer experience and the company's bottom line, but also enhances the lives of employees by complementing and replacing norms, and furthers science as more collaborative, open and global.[3] Unfortunately, only 11% of global Chief Marketing Officers believe that they have completed their digital transformation.[4] Therefore, this book focuses on practical tools and frameworks that readers can apply in the technology, marketing, strategy, structure and cultural aspects of their organization, no matter the size or industry.

Who are we to share insights with you about this challenge? As business professors in marketing and organizational behavior, we have consulted several companies, both separately and together as part of the DATA (Digital, Analytics, Technology and Automation) Initiative at Northeastern University. We analyzed and published research on metrics and big data, organizational growth pains, social media and mobile shopping behavior, and how to nurture data-driven decision making. We wrote books on both the methods and the implementation of digital transformation, as we realized already a decade ago that "It's not the Size of the Data, It's How You Use It" (notsizedata.com). Since that time, we have interacted across four continents with hundreds of managers, analysts and data scientists as executive education and MBA instructors, and in positions such as the President of the American Marketing Association Academic Council and the Vice President of Practice for the Information Systems and Management Science Organization. Our clients include global brands, fast-growing startups, consumer and business product and service providers, big tech firms and media companies. For this book alone, we interviewed dozens of senior data scientists and managers, many of whom gave us permission to share the full interview in Chapter 8. Totaling over a century of combined experience, they work in such industries as apparel, construction, ethics and data literacy consultancy, furniture, lingerie, software services, sports and technology. One central question kept coming back: how do we "break the wall" in digital transformation by democratizing digital data and insights and embedding this learning in our organization?

The answers to this central question led us to seven big insights, which form the basis for the structure of this book:

(1) Start with the vision and integrative framework for digital transformation (Chapter 2).

(2) Adopt a comprehensive and dynamic process for setting relevant business goals of your transformation (Chapter 3).

(3) Identify the gaps through deep analysis of your current situation (Chapter 4).

(4) Hire the right new talent and upgrade current talent (Chapter 5).

(5) Align moving parts of management, information technology (IT) and business in your culture (Chapter 6).

(6) Implement by democratizing digital tools and manage for expectations (Chapter 7).

(7) Learn from others' experiences across industries and job titles (Chapter 8).

The first insight is eloquently expressed by our interviewed data literacy expert Rahul Bhargava:

> *In digital transformation the agency is on digital, not on the thing being transformed. But when you integrate something there are two parties. What is the other one in your case? I would encourage you to think about that question because you could have a lot of answers that are all valid, but which one you care about most can guide you into a terminology that better reflects your ideas and what's the thing being transformed.*

Second, on explicit and business relevant goals, Jon Hay of the Red Sox told us:

> *Sometimes, especially in the IT world people get distracted by shiny objects and find that there's a really interesting challenge that will take a long time, but maybe not be that impactful. I think part of my job as the president in the department is to have those frank conversations: "Here are other things that are coming from people in your department, or adjacent to you. How do we think about what the priority order is? And by the way, how can we maybe align some of these things for more efficiency?"*

Third, analyzing gaps came back in multiple interviews:

> *Sometimes people do not know what they should be looking for, they have tons of dashboards shared but don't know where to start. They are not clear on which dashboard or tool should be used. They've got three BI tools, one of them has 80% of the data, the other one has 15% of that data and the other one has 10% with different overlaps. Data needs to get filtered and sorted to where it is coming from, the trust issues around the data need to be solved.*

Fourth, you can't make an omelet without breaking some eggs. Although many leaders seek the benefits of digital transformation, they are not prepared to pay the costs. These costs typically consist of training existing talent and hiring new, specialized talent. One interviewee told us:

When I'm hiring, I'm filling a very specific need because we want to build out the department. I'm looking for someone that can do a very specific thing very well and that's where it starts to get tricky. Our industry doesn't always pay well but had some perks, which have become less valuable with the pandemic. Now you're competing for technical talent that knows what they're worth, and they can go to literally anywhere, regardless of location. It's actually been an effort for us to convince our senior executives – "Hey look, if you want these sorts of people, to hire data architects you gotta pay market rate."

Fifth, aligning different parts of the organization is key, as shown for ethical issues by Cansu Canca, Founder & Director, of the AI Ethics Lab:

I think now, finally, organizations/companies are realizing that there are ethical issues and they have to deal with them, preferably from the beginning. But I can still not say that they are doing it right. I think the good part is that now there's more awareness. They are putting in place dedicated teams, so that is a big plus. Previously it was only grassroots, and that didn't go anywhere because the leadership was not interested. Now, there is an interest from the leadership and there's grassroots interest. And they are trying. I mean, I think both of these aspects, both the leadership and the grassroots are coming together.

While Rahul Bhargava noted:

When I think about power, I think about the ability to authentically engage and change the circumstances for oneself or for a community that they're involved in. That typically for me is trying to democratize rather than centralize power. If we look at most businesses that have succeeded in various forms of what one calls digital adoption or transformation, they often have a combination of top-down and bottom-up approaches. When you see things like rich media document editing 30 years ago or smartphones, they are two examples that came more from the bottom-up approach where people brought those tools into the workplace and the workplace adapted to support and augment and take partial ownership of those tools to the point where you'll see mobile tool adoption from the top down and you'll see it pushed from the bottom up.

Sixth, it is important to implement by democratizing digital tools and manage for expectations:

I like things where you have a giant screen in the same room where a lot of people are working on the same thing being represented on the screen. So, there's like a shared ownership of what feels like a mirror for us and not a window of somebody looking down at us from outside. That mirror is an example of a version that creates a very different narrative. If we're seeing all of our work up there, then there's a sense of shared ownership that could be cultivated. So sometimes there's like social changes that are very small that work within business language and structure and then having something that talks about that not in a punitive way, but like, oh okay, here's a trend we're seeing, help me understand this trend. But not here's a trend we're seeing you need to work harder on. So much of it is just social.

Finally, it is so much cheaper to learn from others' experiences (successes and failures) than from your own! Therefore, we share with you the insights from executives in the midst of digital transformation in transcripts of the top 10 interviews in Chapter 8.

Let's start the journey!

KEY TAKEAWAYS

Are you aiming to:

(1) Get measurable results from your digital transformation efforts?
(2) Align top management, IT and business leaders in your organization?

(3) Democratize the use of digital tools and opportunities across your company?

(4) Understand and apply a coherent framework for digital transformation?

Have you experienced:

(1) Resistance against digital transformation in your organization?

(2) Recruiting and retention issues of top talent?

(3) Low return on investment from buying digital tools and hiring data scientists?

(4) Frustration with the slow pace of progress toward the digital transformation goals?

Then this book is for you!

NOTES

1. Fitzgerald, M., Kruschwitz, N., Bonnet, D., & Welch, M. (2014). Embracing digital technology: A new strategic imperative. *MIT Sloan Management Review, 55*(2), 2.

2. From Verhoef, P. C., Broekhuizen, T., Bart, Y., Bhattacharya, A., Dong, J. Q., Fabian, N., & Haenlein, M. (2021). Digital transformation: A multidisciplinary reflection and research agenda. *Journal of Business Research, 122,* 889–901.

3. Kraus, S., Schiavone, F., Pluzhnikova, A., & Invernizzi, A. C. (2021). Digital transformation in healthcare: Analyzing the current state-of-research. *Journal of Business Research, 123,* 557–567.

4. https://www.media-sense.com/2022/03/01/mediasense-launches-wave-five-of-media-2020-research-only-11-of-global-cmos-confident-that-they-have-completed-digital-transformation-journey/

2

FRAME DIGITAL TRANSFORMATION

As with any important change, it is key to start with the vision: where does your organization want to be in 5–10 years, and how do you get there? The first question usually evokes imagining how the desired results would look, while the second leads managers to think about what needs to happen for the vision to materialize and various obstacles, ranging from organizational (which users and what are their requirements) to technical (which model and how to validate it?). For instance, in Analytic Dashboards,[1] the vision can be

> *a dashboard at every manager's fingertips, which shows what has happened, allows digging deep into why it has happened and indicates how the user should act by easy what-if analyses based on validated models linking the user's action to key performance indicators.*

In this case, the vision for digital transformation often includes:

(1) Digital business transformation with measurable long-term profit results.
(2) Coherent framework to align top management, information technology and business leaders.
(3) Use of digital tools and opportunities across the company (break the wall!).

Typical obstacles for digital transformation mentioned by the interviewees and identified in our own research and experiences, include:

(4) Resistance against digital transformation.
(5) Recruiting and retention of top talent.
(6) Slow pace, low return on investment and ethical issues with digital transformation.

Digital transformation is as important as ever. In the 2021 Chief Marketing Officer (CMO) survey, a majority of companies report moving past a nascent phase (9% vs 31% in 2020) to an emerging phase with non-integrated digital elements (53%). Unfortunately, only a minority believes to have achieved integration (27%) or even institutionalization (11%). Likewise, academic research on digital transformation is now two decades in, with a recent review distinguishing three groups: (1) digital business transformation, (2) technology as a driver of digital transformation and (3) institutional and societal implications. While top management and information support systems are key, organizations have to rapidly adapt digital transformation and can use the participatory process model to do so.[2] Indeed, our key premise in this book is that top management and business units have their important, but distinct responsibilities and also the speed of processes. Basically, business units and top management adapt to digital transformation together, and are running on two different, but interlocking gears:

In these nested processes, business units invent, experiment and test, while the larger, slower levels, such as information systems and the Top Management Team (TMT) stabilize and conserve accumulated memory of the system dynamics (Fig. 2.1). In this way, the slower and larger levels set the conditions within which faster and smaller ones function. In turn, the smaller wheels need to spin hard and fast in order to drive the larger levels to adapt their vision based on the realities of the business. We call this *nested adaptive cycles (NAC)*.

Our NAC framework is inspired by the below ecological model that tries to understand resilience in the biological

Fig. 2.1.   Nested Components of an Organization.

world by looking at continuous and nesting adaptation cycles of species (Fig. 2.2).

Each level is changing – albeit at differing speeds – all the time: from birth, growth and maturation, to death and renewal.

Fig. 2.2.   Ecological Model of Nesting Adaptation of Species.

We adapt this biological model to the organizational change realities of:

(1) Initiation of change.
(2) Implementation of change.
(3) Building resilience.
(4) Reconsideration and renewal.

As the whole system of interconnected units develop resilience, we expect, even hope, for several occurrences: More often than not, adaptive changes are sparked at the smallest, nimblest part of the system and then cascade up. Parts of the organization that touch the outside world will be first to sense a need, try and adapt to it, and, as the needs grow, the smaller part will revolt and cause a larger change and growth cycle in the neighboring/nesting organizational level. With this cascading implementation of needed changes, the organization builds value and resilience. As the lower levels fully capture the value from these changes, the strategic view from the higher levels will act as a feedback cycle to regroup, reconsider and renew the way lower levels function.

Failure to understand this process leads to many of the issues we encountered in our research and consultancy. These issues form the structure of this book, with each chapter offering a specific solution.

First, the *business objective* of digital transformation may be unclear throughout the organization: *why are we initiating this change and how will it benefit us?* – not just the company but also our day-to-day decisions, either by reducing the time it takes to make them and/or by improving the outcome. In the words of the data literacy expert we interviewed:

> When a business wants to work with data, it's usually thinking about how to use data to measure this person's performance and evaluate it. Instead, I think: how can I help this person use data to do their job better so when you roll out a data initiative, people are not like "Oh no, I don't want to collect that data, you're going to use it to fire me!" – why would anybody participate in this?

Likewise, the Head of Data Governance of a large organization told us:

I work across 40 or 50 different teams and vertical groups to make sure that everyone has a clear, lateral view of what success means and how it's being defined and understood across different groups, making sure that we're holding those people accountable.

In many organizations, change never gets off the ground, due to either a lack of business unit buy-in or enduring top management support. Too often, employees don't see how digital transformation will benefit their own careers, while leaders fail to appreciate the intensity of the process and the far-reaching implications for their competitive position. Chapter 3 dives deeper into how to set the right business objective to initiate change.

Second, how do we overcome the gap between the current and the desired status of digital transformation? As visualized in our digital transformation framework, it is the *interaction* between changes at different levels of the organization that drive the true success of digital transformation. In Chapter 4, we discuss how to unleash the new strategic options that will leverage this interaction to drive value, how to select, nurture and maintain talent in digital transformation and how to reevaluate existing product and customer journeys.

Third, how do you *build the resilience for* this change? It's all about the human element, both individually and as a community. Therefore, our fifth and sixth chapters cover talent and culture, respectively. Chapter 5 explains how to recruit and train the talent to make digital transformation happen. Chapter 6 dives deep into the culture of your organization – both how your existing culture influences how to approach digital transformation, and how digital transformation in turn will influence your culture.

Finally, the vision for digital transformation only materializes when you succeed in bringing it all together as organization-wide reconsideration and renewal. Together with successes, Chapter 7 addresses the implementation challenges in organizations moving toward integration and institutionalization of digital transformation. We have seen numerous organizations design well-intentioned digital transformation plans, only to stumble in this phase.

After our synthesis of observed pitfalls and suggested solutions, it is time to give the floor to our wonderful interviewees for their direct perspective in Chapter 8. They experienced the digital transformation journey in the trenches of dozens of organizations across many different industries. We could not think about a better way to conclude this book than to give them the final word.

KEY TAKEAWAYS

Our vision for successful digital transformation is NAC, where business units invent, experiment and test in fast gears, while the larger and slower interlocking gears of information systems and the TMT stabilize and conserve accumulated memory of the system dynamics. Each has its important, but distinct responsibilities to help the organization go through these stages of digital transformation:

(1) Initiation of change.
(2) Implementation of change.
(3) Building resilience.
(4) Reconsideration and renewal.

NOTES

1. Pauwels, K. (2014). *It's not the size of the data – It's how you use it: Smarter marketing with analytics and dashboards*. Amacom.

2. Walker, B., Holling, C. S., Carpenter, S. R., & Kinzig, A. (2004). Resilience, adaptability and transformability in social–ecological systems. *Ecology and Society, 9*(2), 5–13.

3

SET YOUR GOALS

In Chapter 1, we learned how vision is critical to setting the right goals for digital transformation. This is Chapter 2's "big wheel" that ultimately sets and maintains the other wheels in motion. As you remember, the CEO had hired plenty of data scientists and followed our advice to ensure close cooperation with business decision makers. These wheels were turning, but lacked the needed direction: "What are our swimming lanes?," "Where is the strategic vision?" and "How is leadership ensuring the whole organization is properly challenged on data-driven decision making"? Once a particular problem appears "solved," another issue or obstacle pops up.

This is why our digital transformation framework is inspired by an ecological model describing resilience in the biological world. Often, the actual motives driving organizational transformation are hard to parse, similar to how the purpose of various adaptations species undergo in the natural world remains opaque to an outside observer until much later in the cycle. In contrast with living organisms, businesses can increase their chances of survival and growth by figuring out the right goals of organizational transformation and then pursuing them diligently, rather than just adapting to changing market conditions. The goal of this chapter is to lift that opaque veil and offer actionable advice on how to set effective digital transformation goals in your organization, so that you can win over less focused competition. To start, we'll look at common mistakes companies make when setting goals and why they happen. We then describe three stages of digital transformation, what happens if businesses start with digital transformation before setting goals (spoiler alert – it never ends well!) and suggest how to set the right goals.

Prior to examining the potential goals of digital transformation, it is important to consider the risks of digital transformation becoming a goal in itself rather than being a means for improving a strategic objective for an organization. During our interviews, we learned that the focus often shifts from "why do we need this digital transformation?" to onboarding various data-driven platforms and technologies as fast as possible. The reason is simple – technological innovations over the past few decades have completely reshaped perceptions of how the most valuable companies should behave. In 1995, the Fortune 500 list was dominated by GE, Exxon, AT&T, Coca-Cola and Walmart. Fast forward 25 years, and the list is dominated exclusively by technology companies (Alphabet, Amazon, Apple, Meta and Microsoft) that have mastered leveraging digital technologies to create value. Hence, digital transformation is crucial to a company's growth, if not survival.

COMMON MISTAKES: FEAR OF MISSING OUT ON DIGITAL TRANSFORMATION

In our interviews, we find that corporate executives often succumb to this logical fallacy – that since most successful companies prosper because of some kind of digital transformation, any kind of digital transformation they initiate at their firm would eventually lead to similar success and personal rewards. Managers are often eager to pursue digital transformation because they don't want to get left behind, and because they think this type of transformation has intrinsic value in itself, instead of focusing on finding out how they can use it for something specific and important to their companies. As a result, executives hurry to launch digital transformation initiatives in their companies before they know what they need to transform, why they need to transform, what they are supposed to accomplish, how these outcomes should be measured and what processes they ought to improve.

There is a major problem with this approach: the profitability of such digital transformation efforts is rarely questioned. While certain organizations (especially start-ups at the early stages) may benefit from signaling to their key stakeholders their technical proficiency by adopting nascent digital technologies early, such efforts without clear organizational objectives aligned with profiting from such technologies often fail in the long run.

However, external pressure can and does play a role in organizations adopting digital technologies very quickly. Consumers have been forced to switch online during the pandemic, and many companies have responded accordingly. In the 2020 McKinsey Global Survey, many executives reported that their firms had accelerated their digitization of customer interactions and internal operations by three to four years, accompanied by a sharp rise in the share of digital products in their portfolios. While most of these digital investments were made to address immediate, and often rather short term, tactical objectives, some managers have been leveraging these investments to improve strategic competitiveness as well. To do that, they looked at this fast and large shift to digital as a natural experiment – essentially, a study in which people are exposed to nature's experimental conditions. By analyzing how different stakeholders have reacted to this shift (mostly customers and employees), one can gain insights that can help shape strategy and foster the advancement of digital transformation.

Turning now to the data analytics side of digital transformation, we find that many organizations focused on becoming driven by data commit a similar mistake – collecting data for the sake of data collection. This idea is often connected with the infamous quote from GigaOM industry conference in 2013, where the CIA's chief technology officer, Ira "Gus" Hunt, said:[1]

> *The value of any piece of information is only known when you can connect it with something else that arrives at a future point in time …. Since you can't connect dots you don't have, it drives us into a mode of fundamentally trying to collect everything and hang on to it forever.*

While attractive in theory, this is not only completely impractical these days, given the sheer volume of data that keeps exponentially increasing, but may also backfire. For example, in the context of behavioral targeting, research[2] shows that, since the most personalized ads are less effective because consumers may worry they are being exploited, businesses may be better off collecting less data about them.

Further, firms often become overwhelmed by the volume and variety of data they are ingesting every day (or every second, in data-intensive industries), and start prioritizing how to utilize these data for the organization, deciding on internal goals and motivating related executives accordingly. This orientation to becoming "data-driven," in the sense of "we build systems to maximize the value of capturing and processing relevant data" is not only prone to becoming a race against time where a company keeps running just to remain in the same place (since the volume and variety of relevant data keep increasing over time), but also liable to fail to deliver actionable or timely insights.

Companies often fail to realize the time-sensitive nature of data value: managers are often convinced that collecting more data will improve the accuracy of their machine learning models. However, recent research[3] found that when data lose relevance over time, it may be optimal to collect a limited amount of recent data instead of keeping around an infinite supply of older (less relevant) data. The inclusion of older datasets can even hurt models' accuracy, so having more data creates more value only if companies remember to delete older, less relevant data. Because of this, businesses must dynamically balance the stock of historical data against the flow of new data. This is especially true for more established firms, as they are more likely to have collected a lot of historical data.

In addition to the volume-time tradeoff, firms usually overlook the need to pay attention to the quality of their data. When the data quality is low, even in an ideal case of obtaining and processing lots of relevant data very fast, the resulting value created from the data will not be great. Last but not least, managers often neglect to gather competitive intelligence on how their competitors prioritize data volume, timeliness and quality. This information may, in turn, shape strategic priorities for data-driven transformation that maximize the company's chances to survive and grow, especially in highly competitive markets. These considerations are not dissimilar to the material–time–quality concept and related considerations arising in competitive chess games.[4]

WHY DO COMPANIES MAKE THESE MISTAKES IN HOW THEY SET GOALS?

One of the reasons for such common mistakes stems from a well-known "Streetlight effect." Such an effect is best illustrated by this joke:

> *A policeman sees a drunk man searching for something under a streetlight and asks what the drunk has lost. He says he lost his keys and they both look under the streetlight together. After a few minutes the policeman asks if he is sure he lost them here, and the drunk replies, no, that he lost them in the park. The policeman asks why he is searching here, and the drunk replies, "this is where the light is."*

Likewise, companies often fall prey to this observational bias and look for solutions to their challenges in places that are easy to find, especially when the market offers them many options for adopting new technologies or adopting a novel data management platform. As a result, an organization is more likely to increase the brightness of the proverbial light, rather than examine where exactly they should "look for keys." In other words, firms typically focus on what problems they can solve and what goals they can achieve given the readily available data and technologies, rather than identifying their most important strategic goals first, before they evaluate whether data and technologies can (or cannot) aid them in achieving these goals. Such behaviors include adopting cloud services off the shelf or deploying digital transformation through the information technology (IT) department.

This problem of over-focusing on accessible (and, often, short term and tactical) rather than on pertinent strategic goals is further exacerbated by two factors. First, measuring short-term, tactical deployment of digital transformation instruments is simply easier, compared with assessing metrics corresponding to longer-term strategic goals. Second, managerial incentives may not be well aligned with what is best for the company. This is not only because the average tenure of a C-level executive is under five years (according to 2020 Korn Ferry study), suggesting potentially misaligned incentives when it comes to long-term value creation. It is also because executing a digital transformation that fulfills short-term goals at the cost of sacrificing long-term company success may bring the senior executive in charge necessary recognition and demonstrated (short term) results that would increase their immediate personal marketability, often resulting in that executive getting recruited by another company, before longer-term results start showing why the performed digital transformation may have been quite myopic.

Unfortunately, the harm suffered by a firm in the aftermath of such a myopic transformation performed for short-term gains often may have long-lasting negative consequences. What we commonly see across multiple industries is that company executives tend to pursue and onboard new digital technologies as a result of relying on first-order thinking without using second-order thinking. For example, adding a new digital channel may benefit a strong traditional retail brand in the short term (first-order thinking) through saving on service costs, but, at the same time, encouraging loyal customers to transact digitally may reduce brand attitudes and increase the likelihood of customer poaching by digital-only competitors in the longer term (second-order thinking). This idea stems from Chesterton's Fence principle, described by G. K. Chesterton as follows:

> There exists in such a case a certain institution or law; let us say, for the sake of simplicity, a fence or gate erected across a road. The more modern type of reformer goes gaily up to it and says, "I don't see the use of this; let us clear it away." To which the more intelligent type of reformer will do well to answer: "If you don't see the use of it, I certainly won't let you clear it away. Go away and think. Then, when you can come back and tell me that you do see the use of it, I may allow you to destroy it."

Sadly, it is not often that senior company executives looking to "clear fences" in pursuit of digital transformation are confronted by a "more intelligent type" of a company stakeholder.

THREE STAGES OF DIGITAL TRANSFORMATION

Before we examine how companies may improve the better ways in which they could strategically set up digital transformation goals, it is important to define first what we mean by digital transformation. We define it as *a change in how a firm employs digital technologies, to develop a new digital business model that helps to create and appropriate more value for the firm.*[5] Several external factors often drive the need for digital transformation, including the prevalence of big data and emerging digital technologies, as well as the rise of data-rich competitors that blur traditional industry lines. But, most importantly, the impact of digital technologies on consumer behavior has reached every stage of the customer decision-making process, from educating them about existing offerings to enabling them to co-create new products with companies.

Many companies limit their digital transformation activities to the first two stages, consisting mostly of tactical elements – digitization and digitalization. Typically, digitization refers to the conversion of analog information into a digital format for storage, processing, transmission and enabling the use of computational resources. Digitization of order processes, internal accounting documents and consumer surveys are examples of digitization. In practice, digitization primarily affects internal and external documentation processes, without changing value-creating processes.

Digitalization is the process of modifying existing business processes through the application of IT or digital technologies. A good example is the introduction of new digital communication channels that allow all customers to connect easily with firms and each other, thereby changing traditional interactions between firms and their customers. IT is a key enabler of digitalization through which business processes, such as communication, distribution and business relationship management, can be reimagined. In the process of digitalization, companies utilize digital technologies to optimize existing business processes by integrating new sociotechnical structures, allowing them to better coordinate their processes, and creating additional customer value by enhancing user experiences. Digitalization is not only about reducing costs, but may also enhance customer experiences.

Strategic digital transformation differs from this in that it involves implementing new business logic to create and capture value. A transformation of this sort affects the company as a whole and its way of doing business, going beyond simple changes in organizational processes. The aim is to modify the business logic and value creation processes of a company. By bringing together data analytics and digital technologies to enable more agile interactions with suppliers, customers and competitors, the ultimate goal of strategic digital transformation is to achieve a competitive advantage by leveraging existing core competencies or developing new ones. For example, once statistical analysis had transformed the capacity to hire effective players at the Red Sox, they began deploying the same talent and methods to operations, greatly improving revenue yield at games. At Victoria's Secret, new data sources and analytics are leveraged to improve servicing of customers at both brick-and-mortar stores and online touchpoints, demonstrating to channel managers that the overall goal is to enhance customer value rather than displace one channel with another.

Incumbent firms should pay special attention to strategic digital transformation. Due to legacy issues, it is often difficult for incumbent companies to search and implement business model innovations for digital transformation. It is not uncommon for them to have to deal with conflicts and trade-offs between existing and new business practices. When moving to digital, existing business models may need to change significantly, leading to their obsolescence. As an incumbent business gradually transforms its traditional model into a digital one, they may start with minor tactical changes (e.g., digitization or digitalization). The process usually begins with small teams whose members are jacks of all trades with the inherent ability to collaborate across departmental and hierarchical boundaries. As people become accustomed to the benefits of digital transformation, they are more likely to trust analysts and data scientists.

WHAT HAPPENS WHEN COMPANIES START DIGITAL TRANSFORMATION BEFORE SETTING GOALS INTERNALLY?

Our interviews indicate that firms often begin digital transformation before setting internal goals. To illustrate how this typically plays out in practice, put yourself in the shoes of such a typical executive – what happens next? When you do not have the basic building blocks necessary to move forward, you begin looking for and inviting people who claim to know how to digitally transform your business and are fluent in related terminology, such as consultants and software vendors. Now, keep in mind that you are still under the illusion that the only thing your company needs to succeed is digital transformation, the faster the better. Soon enough, you realize that these external stakeholders are driving the entire transformation process inside your company without having a clue about the underlying company-specific processes they are altering. No wonder such stories often result in failure, leading company executives to step back and ask themselves – why did we not win from this digital transformation, what went wrong?

The key takeaway from this story is not that businesses should never use consultants and software vendors to help them during their digital transformation journeys, but rather to emphasize the importance of setting the right type of goals before embarking on these journeys. What is common for many companies that succeeded by undergoing digital transformation is that they started by asking the right questions: What are the processes that would serve our relevant stakeholders critical for value creation (customers, partners and vendors) better by being digital? How do we transform those processes to be more effective and efficient? And then, how do we build that into a scalable structure in our organization, so that we can perform these incremental improvements faster and more often?

PROCESS FOR SETTING RIGHT GOALS

As we look back on the history of digital transformation, companies often turned to an inefficient analog process to see how they could optimize it using available digital technologies. For example, back in the 1990s many firms adopted the Internet to improve both internal and external communication. As most digital technologies have been getting better and cheaper over time, companies have identified thousands of such process-improving opportunities that create value by making happier stakeholders (primarily consumers and employees), improving efficiency, gaining competitive advantage, reducing costs or through some combination of these.

As firms pursued such opportunities one by one, they gained efficiencies at each step, and that effectively achieved their digital transformation. At this point, however, many company executives consider hundreds, and some may even be considering thousands, of processes that may be able to benefit from being digitally transformed – how do you prioritize all these potential opportunities? What if you choose the "wrong" ones to change first?

In our interview, Neil Hoyne, Chief Measurement Strategist at Google, argues that companies would get infinitely more value from building and understanding the ongoing, underlying strategic process (the "big wheel" from our guiding framework) by which they can transform their organization, compared with the value that could be obtained through tactics (individual process-improvement opportunities, or "small wheels"):

> *Technology will continue to bring new ways to interact with customers. We've moved from email to chatbots, to live agent support, to machine learning predictions and interventions. These transformations will keep happening, and digital technology will keep making it easier to improve processes. Considering that, CEOs need to realize that success won't be determined by the first one to five or ten individual process changes. Instead, you should be thinking: can you build a scalable process? This way, you can leverage the latest technologies as they come out and get more efficiencies from your business. It's the challenge*

and diversity of the tactics that I recommend focusing on, not the initial opportunity. When a CEO says it's an important transformation, it's something big and visible in the organization. It'll be different than when an individual analyst just wants to improve their process. And I think the key is to keep on growing a collection of these individual process improvements – not just focusing on measuring the outcomes of these discrete efforts, but to ask: What did we learn about these transformations? What did we learn in terms of approvals? In terms of timing? What are the gaps when it comes to vendor or product support that we need to fill? And then, keep repeating that process over time. This is, in my opinion, a much better overarching goal than, say, simply concentrating on how much growth you would be able to achieve with one or two best currently available tactics.

While some of the goals of digital transformation may be to simplify and streamline how a firm conducts its operations, the process itself can be far from easy – for example, a 2020 Boston Consulting Group study found that over 70% of digital transformation projects fall short of their goals. The rest of this book will provide the roadmap on how managers can move from setting goals to successful digital transformation executions.

KEY TAKEAWAYS

(1) Ensure digital transformation does not become a goal in itself for your organization.

(2) Always question the profitability of digital transformation in the long term.

(3) Never collect any data just for the sake of data collection.

(4) Dynamically balance the stock of historical data against the flow of new data.

(5) Balance trade-offs across data volume, timeliness and quality to win against competition.

(6) Focus on pertinent long-term goals, not just measurable, accessible and short-term goals.

(7) Don't break processes unless you know why they exist (Chesterton's Fence principle).
(8) Take care of digitization, digitalization and strategic digital transformation.
(9) Beware of starting digital transformation before setting your own goals internally.
(10) Prioritize building the strategic learning process over optimizing individual processes.

NOTES

1. https://www.businessinsider.com/cia-presentation-on-big-data-2013-3

2. Gardete, P. M., & Bart, Y. (2018). Tailored cheap talk: The effects of privacy policy on ad content and market outcomes. *Marketing Science, 37*(5), 733–752.

3. Valavi, E., Hestness, J., Ardalani, N., & Iansiti, M. (2022). Time and the value of data. arXiv preprint:2203.09118.

4. Kasparov, G. (2007). *How life imitates chess: Making the right moves, from the Board to the Boardroom.* Bloomsbury USA: Arrow Books.

5. From Verhoef, P. C., Broekhuizen, T., Bart, Y., Bhattacharya, A., Dong, J. Q., Fabian, N., & Haenlein, M. (2021). Digital transformation: A multidisciplinary reflection and research agenda. *Journal of Business Research, 122,* 889–901.

4

ANALYZE THE GAPS

Digital transformation is a journey that differs for each organization. All the interviewed experts talked about the need for customization. Industries, such as apparel, construction, furniture, lingerie, software services and sports, face different customer needs and competitive pressures. Most importantly, each organization has its own objectives, culture, structure and obstacles. For the CEO in our opening example, the overfocus on data and data scientists prevented leadership from reimagining the value the company could provide to customers through digital transformation and redesigning the human resources to support this new value.

Therefore, we highly recommend starting with a gap analysis. Following our nested adaptive cycles (NAC) framework, this concerns both the gap in how businesses interact with customers (the small and fast turning wheels) and the gap in how top leadership is thinking about change management in the context of digital transformation. Therefore, in this chapter, we offer tried-and-true approaches to:

(1) Reevaluate product and customer journeys for digitalization.
(2) Develop and execute the architecture to support this new journey.

REEVALUATE PRODUCT AND CUSTOMER
JOURNEYS FOR DIGITALIZATION

Amazon is famous for its culture of working backwards from the customer, demanding any new initiative is first written as a PR/FAQ, that is, a press release (how the final product/service would be like for the customer) followed by frequently asked questions about why and how the organization can deliver this new customer experience, starting from its current situation.[1] We recommend a similar approach to envisioning how digital transformation will improve product and customer journeys.

Working backwards from the customer implies a focus on customer needs in both the value proposition (Product and Price) and how they want to obtain and learn about this value (Place and Promotion in the 4Ps of the marketing mix). For instance, Victoria's Secret realized that many consumers started feeling comfortable ordering even new products online but still enjoyed personalization. As a result, the company started A/B testing of new products and of personalization options. Thus, organizations need to reevaluate product and customer journeys to explore where digital can transform (simplify or optimize) existing processes. The solution could be incremental or quite radical.

First, *incremental* solutions involve swapping out analog activities with digital ones. Take cruise ships, for example. Two of this book's authors loved the trip itself, including lodging, entertainment options and the daily stops at gorgeous islands, but hated getting on and off the ship. The process was lengthy and uncomfortable. In 2018, Caribbean Cruise Lines deployed microservices as part of an Agile methodology in its digital transformation.[2] The resulting faster disembarkation process saved passengers hours of standing in line. Another example comes from business-to-business customer call centers, which often require engineers to solve complex problems. A company we consulted saved millions of expensive engineering time with a machine learning model that classified incoming complaints, and connected the engineers with solutions to analogous issues. As an added bonus, the system improves over time thanks to engineer feedback (was the suggested solution appropriate and did it solve the problem?) and is a wonderful tool to onboard new engineers. You too can use digital transformation to fix processes customers are unhappy with. The key is to look for any opportunities to save money, time and people in serving customers.

Second, more *radical* solutions rethink the full customer journey to better serve the needs of today's customers. For instance, PayPal was always delayed due to the necessary legal approval, which took time. Because time was of the essence to its customers, the company merged its separate divisions for payments and compliance into one entity. A favorite example predating digital is Cirque du Soleil, started in 1984 by former street performers Guy Laliberte and Gille Ste-Croix. Its theatrical, character-driven stories and spectacular acrobatics redefined the traditional circus, with its omnipresence of performing animals, which were both expensive and whose (ab)use raised ethical issues.

The more radical the solution, the greater the cost over status quo, but also the greater the chance to increase sales at every stage of the journey. You can digitally transform the "upper funnel" by building awareness, the "mid funnel" by profiling and targeting specific prospects and the "lower funnel" by making purchase and payment as easy as possible. Amazon.com started out with the latter, becoming the most convenient way to find and buy products consumers were already actively looking for. When they opened up their marketplace to other brands, they also started to offer lower-funnel advertising to do the same: sponsored products helped consumers find the brand's product they were looking for. Over time, Amazon started offering mid-funnel advertising, such as sponsored brands, allowing sellers to showcase their range of products and build brand consideration. Moreover, "remarketing" tools help brands to bring back consumers that visited the product's detail page. Nowadays, brands can build awareness through streaming ads (via Fire TV or IMdB), audio ads (via Alexa), online video and display throughout the Internet. Artificial intelligence (AI) and predictive analytics help to reach potential customers and target campaigns by geography and consumer behavior.

How can you start to reevaluate product and customer journeys? First, walk in the shoes of your customers: try yourself to order from your company and experience by yourself the typical steps, bottlenecks and (hopefully) points of delight. Second, customer journey maps are a widely available tool for visualizing the steps in a typical consumer journey. This helps your team to understand jobs-to-do at every stage and to rethink how this customer need could be met better, faster or with less headache. Key elements of such customer journey maps include:

Touchpoints – *what* customers *do* while interacting and *how* they do it.

Channels – *where* they perform actions (e.g., review sites, online retail, social media).

Thoughts and feelings – what the customer thinks and feels at each touchpoint.

Not every potential customer has the same journey, so maps often use personas (representing customer segments) and scenarios to illustrate different entry points and journey progressions. For instance, busy financial directors (like Steven Harvey) could be persuaded to buy and play your strategy videogame, but his decision journey is likely to be long and uncertain (Fig. 4.1)

While very busy at work and sharing his free time with his fiancée, Steven remembers how much fun he used to have thinking and making strategies. An ad, game review, editorial or friend can make him aware of your new game. Steven then looks it up in the Appstore, where he checks the art, the star rating, the reviews and price to make up his mind. Even though he prefers your game, he might still not end up purchasing it because other activities take

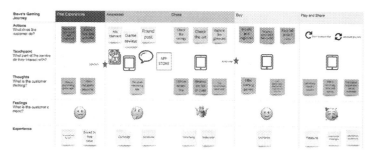

Fig. 4.1. Customer Journey of Genre Gamer.

priority for a while. And after purchase, our busy Steven still needs time to play it and appreciate both the relaxation as the challenge of a good game. Finally, he may end up inviting his friends and/ or sharing his experience on social media and with a star rating. Therefore, as long as your product fits Steven's need, your make-or-break marketing needs to focus on awareness and actual play.

Obviously, this customer journey map would look very different for a middle-schooler who plays videogames for hours a day and tries several new ones each week. Let's call him Mir. Mir typically becomes aware of new games through the macro-influencers he follows on Twitch and YouTube. Moreover, he subscribes to get notifications of his favorite game developers, even a year before the game is actually launched! While he is not as time-sensitive as Steven, he is much more price-sensitive, because he either has to buy the game with his limited allowance, or convince his parents that the game is "educational" so they will partially fund it. Once bought, the game is almost certain to enjoy multiple hours of Mir's playing time, both by himself and in a multiplayer online environment, thus jumpstarting direct network effects. However, he is hard to impress and unlikely to recommend your title to his favorite gamer girl – only a few games a year make the cut. To help move Mir's customer journey along, your marketing needs to include key influencers, keep trial prices low (e.g., with a freemium or ad-supported business model) and motivate Mir to rate the game and share it with friends if he likes it.

Customer journey maps often use the "purchase funnel" or "consumer decision journey" as a starting point: customers start with the recognition of a need and/or becoming aware of a solution (e.g., a prescription drug for their ailment), then educate themselves about alternatives (e.g., your brand) and develop a preference for the chosen alternative, which they then experience to their (dis)satisfaction and repeat purchase. Often, their experiences also reach other potential customers as reviews or word-of-mouth, which is easily expressed and accessed in the digital space. However, it is important not to limit your research to online, and definitely not to a single online channel. Recent research has demonstrated different information from online and offline metrics of the customer journey, with online metrics changing much faster than your performance, and survey-measured attitudes changing slower, but predicting your performance better in the long run. Therefore, in addition to the "fast lane" of online customer behavior (DO), it remains important to learn what customers KNOW and FEEL in the slowly changing attitude lanes[3] (Fig. 4.2).

It is the combination of these fast and slow lanes that allows you to properly measure, interpret and influence the different influences in the customer journey.

Awareness and consideration are typically assessed in surveys, using samples representative of your customer population. The more aware potential customers are of your brand, the more likely they are to search for it, click on its ads and visits its store or websites. Likewise, these actions also help inform consumers better, thus increasing their consideration for your brand and their feelings (liking and preference). Finally, their purchase and

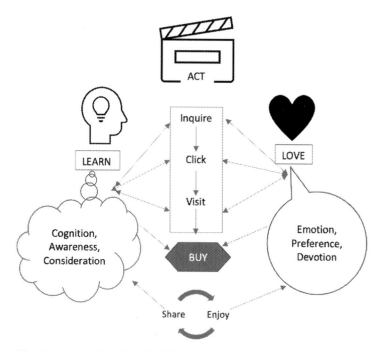

Fig. 4.2.   Integrative Model of Attitudes and Actions.

consumption experience feeds back into their knowledge and loyalty and, if expressed to others, in the thoughts and feelings of the
population of potential customers, checking reviews on Amazon
and brand interactions on social media.

To quantify such a model with data typically available to companies, we often simplify it to the following diamond[4] (Fig. 4.3).

Growth in awareness and consideration (measured in surveys
or Amazon Brand Metrics, for example) goes hand-in-hand with
increased search for your brand – both branded search and click-
throughs when your brand shows up high in organic search. These
in turn lead to more visits – to your online store but also to your
brick-and-mortar store and/or retailers that stock your product.
Finally, purchase and post-purchase metrics can include sales, satisfaction, net promoter score and expressions of (dis)satisfaction
in offline or online word-of-mouth. Managers (and consultants)
differ in their favorite entry point, for example:

(1) Start with building attitudes (upper funnel) so that your
lower-funnel marketing (e.g., paid search and sponsored
products) is more effective.

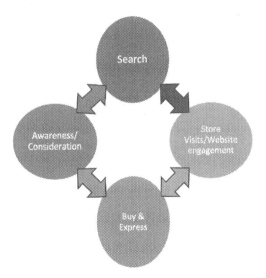

Fig. 4.3.   Customer Diamond Wheel.

(2) Increase your share of search and choose the right keywords to show up high in the search ranking.

(3) Ensure your product's physical availability and prominence in the store, and the rest will follow.

(4) Get your product in the hands of as many consumers as possible (e.g., through free or highly subsidized trial), after which their satisfaction will drive the diamond wheel.

Whichever your favorite, our advice is to also think about which of these transitions is your current "weak link" in the chain:

(1) Do many potential customers not even know you exist (awareness) or do not consider you as a "serious player" in the category (consideration)?

(2) Can aware prospects easily find you when they are searching?

(3) Do your stores and websites make it easy to get information and make a decision?

(4) Is your buying and experience sharing process convenient?

Each of these issues requires a different marketing and management focus, and may lead you to a new way to design your position to drive value in the new strategy. For instance, sports teams were late to the dynamic pricing championed by airlines: until a decade ago, you would pay the same price for many types of seats in Fenway stadium. With the embrace of analytics in sports, customer convenience and flexibility improved, leading to greater revenues for the company.

DEVELOP AND EXECUTE THE ARCHITECTURE TO SUPPORT THE NEW JOURNEYS

Once your organization has designed the vision of the new customer journey, you need to develop and execute the new architecture either in an incremental or a radical manner. Going back to the CEO in our opening example, we heard grumblings from different employees that they lacked clear leadership direction, swimming lanes and resources to execute on the new strategy. As your organization progresses in digital transformation, its outcomes and deliverables greatly depend on how effectively management and communication work together.

Does your firm have a bottom-up management approach? In terms of our NAC framework, do the small wheels typically spin first, forcing the larger wheels into motion? Typically, specialists, who know all the technicalities of their job, will initiate the digital transformation implementation. Often, it will have a very clear and specific application, however, it may lack long-term vision. Therefore, a bottom-up design tends to work well with incremental digital transformation as it improves processes such as customer onboarding or call center complaint management. Hence, the project initiator will need to gain managerial support in the first place. Because it is suggested by process-involved employees, you can anticipate a high level of employee engagement and motivation. However, the project initiator will need to gain senior management support, especially if additional resources are needed and/or if the improved process also affects other parts of the business. In top-performing companies we consulted, employees were empowered to suggest such initiatives through a clear process of writing a supporting document, working backwards from the customer problem or opportunity and explaining the dependencies on other teams for success. Senior management reviews these proposals, consults with related teams and gives feedback and blessing.

In contrast, a top-down management style involves the larger wheel turning and setting the smaller wheels in motion. This typically means that digital transformation enjoys managerial support, but it may lack employee participation and understanding of many practical barriers and bottlenecks. Radical changes, such as business model pivots and payment system switches, are a good fit for a top-down approach. Senior management is convinced this piece to digital transformation is important to the company, and communicates its request to employees, who are invited to critique the execution given their intimate knowledge of the process and, often, of the affected customers. Employees can become motivated if they understand the purpose of digital transformation and which role they have to play in the project.

Managers should also communicate how the project may not just benefit the customer and organization, but also the work and career of the employees themselves. Finally, inviting employee feedback is valuable only if the project specifics can be updated based on this feedback.

We summarize pros and cons of the top-down and bottom-up strategies in Table 4.1.

Today's large organizations rarely apply either of the two approaches in its pure state. The two approaches can coexist and serve different needs of a firm. The blend of the two approaches

Table 4.1.   Top-down and Bottom-up Management Designs: Pros and Cons.

Approach	Top-down	Bottom-up
Project initiator	Senior managers	Specialists, knowledge workers
Pros	• Broad knowledge, experience and ability to see the big picture of the project initiators • Project aligned with the common business strategy and vision • Strategic objectives and goals are determined early in the project	• Specific knowledge of the problem and organizational needs of the project initiators • Flexibility • Highly motivated project team • Employees feel valued, as their opinions and feedback matter • Often less expensive to implement
Cons	• Lack of flexibility • Poor responsiveness • Often incurs higher implementation cost • Potential poor employee participation and motivation • Employees feel their input is not valued	• Lack of long-term vision • Inability of the project initiators to see all factors affecting the problem or company's performance • Lack of managerial support

translates into a powerful merger of vision and strategic thinking of senior managers with creativity and technical skills of specialists – the perfect combination for a dashboard success!

KEY TAKEAWAYS

What is the gap in your current versus desired situation? Our NAC framework reveals action is needed both bottom-up and top-down:

(1) Reevaluate product and customer journeys for digitalization.
(2) Develop and execute the architecture to support this new journey.

Turning the wheels of business requires a radical or incremental rethinking of the customer journey and how it can be improved with digital transformation. Customer journey maps and funnels are often helpful for this exercise, blending customer behavior (e.g., online actions) with their thoughts and feelings (often from asking them). Next, the architecture may be top-down or bottom-up depending on the management style in your organization. Executing this architecture, and overcoming the gaps, requires finding and training the right talent, discussed in the next chapter.

NOTES

1. McLean, W. L. (2021). https://medium.com/intrico-io/strategy-tool-amazons-pr-faq-72b3e49aa167

2. Sweary, R. (2021). https://www.forbes.com/sites/forbestechcouncil/2021/03/05/you-cant-have-a-revolution-every-day-invest-in-incremental-digital-transformation/?sh=60e026923265

3. Adapted from Pauwels, K., & van Ewijk, B. (2013). *Best paper award at the Marketing Science Institute*. https://www.msi.org/working-papers/do-online-behavior-tracking-or-attitude-survey-metrics-drive-brand-

sales-an-integrative-model-of-attitudes-and-actions-on-the-consumer-boulevard/

4. Adapted from Pauwels, K., & van Ewijk, B. (2020). Enduring attitudes and contextual interest: When and why attitude surveys still matter in the online consumer decision journey. *Journal of Interactive Marketing, 52*, 20–34.

5

WIELD THE SLEDGEHAMMER

You've identified your digital transformation goals (Chapter 3) and used the value chain to identify key gaps (Chapter 4). Once you've determined the *goals* and *gaps* relevant to digital transformation, it is time to assemble the team. Circling back to our New York C-suite, we hear the yearning for a team of unicorn data scientists and digital evangelists that take charge of the transformation. Some collective of superhumans that would wield Thor's hammer to break the silos of information in the organization, and bring everyone together in pursuing the new goals, new ways of behaving. That talent might not always be accessible, nor be necessary for your firm.

As we have shared in Chapter 2, due to the interconnectedness of parts of an organization, the transformation efforts will follow a nested adaptive cycle framework. This cycle indeed starts with the individual and cascades through to the whole organization in all its levels. As such, the organization can gain a tremendous amount of efficiency by initiating change through the "right" individuals. The question is, how do we decide who the right people are?

TECHNICAL VERSUS CULTURAL GOALS

Common reasons for digital transformation hiring include a desire to increase sophistication of modeling and machine learning, standardizing data structures and creating dashboards. When you seek true digital transformation, you'll soon realize that the real goal lies beyond specific technical capabilities and encompasses the whole organization. A digitalization dream team will be able to assist in creating an organization-wide culture that amplifies digitalization efforts. It's all too common for managers to ask Human Resources (HR) to find the most qualified candidates in machine learning and data engineering, while forgetting the overall challenge of getting buy-in throughout the entire organization. It's not that technical talent isn't important, it's that we should hire with the overarching transformation goal in mind. The temptation is to make big plans with all the problems of large-scale projects including sunk cost syndrome (i.e., continuing a failing project just because significant investment has already been made) and too-big-to-fail (i.e., a project becoming so overreaching across the organization that letting it fail will be catastrophic). Shifting the focus to include cultural change as an objective makes clear that smaller, yet more widespread and incremental changes can have much greater impact on the bottom line than punctuated showcase projects.

Digital transformation is not an event or series of projects but rather a pervading perspective that values evidence-based ideation and action throughout the organization. In some cases, these changes enhance existing processes such as accelerating the speed at which feedback is obtained from decisions. In other cases, entirely new abilities are possible. When digital structures are widely adopted, this can enable new practices such as iterative experimentation or real-time customer feedback. However, new approaches can sit unused or worse, elicit unwarranted skepticism. Such enhancements are more likely to create value for the firm in the presence of an accompanying cultural norm that welcomes the changes and adaptations that digitalization enables. Hiring efforts should therefore look to emphasize this cultural perspective in addition to selecting for technical prowess. From the perspective of securing talent, achieving this may entail combining team members who are collectively:

(1) cross-disciplinary,
(2) have a balanced knowledge of existing firm fundamentals and new processes,

(3) occupy critical roles in organizational networks, and

(4) possess I- and T-shaped expertise.

In this chapter, we first formulate the criteria to identify the necessary talent, which often means hiring your own and upskilling them in your organization. Next, we discuss the cross-disciplinary, knowledge, organizational networks and I- and T-shaped expertise.

CRITERIA TO IDENTIFY THE NECESSARY TALENT

In pursuing digitalization, the desired traits for new team members may be unfamiliar to the HR department. The obvious requirements include technical capability and a demonstrated ability to broadly communicate complex concepts in a simplified manner, however, the need to find people who can help instill norms supporting *digital culture* within the organization may be less salient. Culture is more than the sum of its parts and hiring individuals with accomplished data science or managerial credentials does not guarantee adoption of the digital culture needed for digital transformation. Especially in legacy institutions, having a credible connection with the existing culture is essential for any change agent to gain trust and create an impact. Team members need to gel with leadership, internalize the transformation goals and play an active role in spreading digital culture.

Taking this perspective, key considerations in finding the members of a digital transformation team are as follows:

- *Leadership complementarity*: Can the person work with the leader(s) driving digital transformation? This includes being a complement to the leader's abilities. If leadership is heavy on management and light on data science, the recruit should be able to transform technical insights into actionable recommendations and managerial insights into technical projects. Conversely, a technically oriented leader may require a lieutenant who can assist in getting buy-in from all areas of the organization. Successful startups often arise from this combination, and successful digital transformation is no exception. If existing leadership realizes the need for complementarity, finding suitable people becomes easier. However, competitive pressures and day-to-day workloads can lead to HR being given a job specification that is overly simplistic in its emphasis on qualifications and experience, without due consideration of how well they will be able to integrate with leadership. If recruiters are unable to determine compatibility, this can lead to wasted interview stages where mistakes become apparent only at the last "meet the leader" phase, or – even costlier – after the change efforts are underway.

- *Skill relevance*: How much technical talent is really needed? Senior data scientists tend to be best at applying advanced approaches to rich datasets. While this may potentially yield inventive insights, the value of these findings to the organizations presupposes the data needed for such modeling is available, and that insights will be appreciated by decision makers throughout the organization. HR needs to be equipped to distinguish between coding and machine learning skills that are effective in isolation versus data skills that can be applied as part of an actionable agenda. Hiring managers should be urged to distinguish "must-haves" from "nice-to-haves" in technical proficiency. Degree qualifications and completed technical projects are often unrelated to the capacity to help a team achieve digital transformation. The challenge for recruiters is that technical qualifications are more easily expressed in resumes and checkboxes on applications. Unfortunately, an emphasis upon these inputs can filter out more relevant candidates.

- *Credibility*: For the change team to succeed, they should be able to wade through the thick molasses of inevitable resistance. They should be able to provide the requisite psychological safety to the members of the organization they are trying to impact. This requires the change agents to be credible in the eyes of the people they are trying to secure buy-in from. Only through this credibility can they gain the level of trust needed to create an environment conducive to learning and experimenting.

How can we help HR find the right people? The full team context must be communicated. Suppose the ideal team requires data analysis, data engineering and data communication, and the needs gap has been identified. In that case, HR can get to work on looking for candidates that can collectively fulfill these roles. Here, we want to emphasize the notion of "collectively" one more time. Allowing HR to consider potential hires in a collective manner can open up hiring strategies that would be impossible in the traditional "candidate by candidate" approach. Such "hiring scrums" are often limited to extreme growth times, but we've had excellent experiences with them also in a digital transformation context. An MBA-type with coding bootcamp experience may be preferred for a data translator role compared to a qualified data scientist with a doctoral degree, yet together two such candidates could be very effective in enacting a digitalized culture. Like a baseball team, a game can just as effectively be won with a combination of talent that collectively exceeds the contribution made by exceptional individual talents. Effective digital transformation is often best served by taking this "moneyball"[1] approach to recruiting. To boot, not competing with other firms for the same "top" unidimensional talent makes the hiring process much more cost-effective.

HIRE THE RIGHT PEOPLE

The race to hire data scientists and assemble data lakes characterized the heady early days of digital transformation. Companies created new teams with big budgets, often stuffed with doctorates in computer science wielding the latest tools in cloud computing. However, this often intimidates incumbent team members and marginalizes the value of any finding. Over time, the resultant class structure inhibited rather than enhanced digital transformation. Firms quickly realized technical acumen better translated into value when accompanied by contextual expertise.

NEW AND EXISTING KNOWLEDGE: HIRE YOUR OWN!

Sticking to your own when trying to achieve dramatic change may seem counterintuitive. After all, isn't resistance often due to incumbent managers and teams? While change is often slowed by existing stakeholders, what's more important is the reason for resistance. Fear of losing relevance and responsibility is entirely justified when new hires arrive. Consider: how many years has it been since most of us took an exam, never mind completing an entire degree that probably didn't exist 10 years ago? Importing new faces with new skills is attractive because it brings a fresh perspective. However, perhaps we should first ask what can be gained by training people who already know how to execute projects and influence the key people in order to get things done. Another way to look at hiring in digital transformation is: How much of what needs to be done requires new skills and techniques versus how much change can be achieved by breaking the data and knowledge walls and putting know-how in the right hands? It may be surprising how little new technical proficiency can achieve without the ability to implement these new approaches (Fig. 5.1).

Of course, the ideal combination may very well be a team with both new and existing members but even then we should ask: "Have I given the people I already have the opportunity to enact change?" But how do we achieve this? Upskilling through boot-camps and certificate programs are examples of intense concen-trated qualifications that can not only build individual technical skills, but also enable employees to form the exact types of intra-company networks that will be needed in digital transformation. A single workshop attended by individuals from finance, information

Fig. 5.1.   New and Existing Knowledge.

technology (IT), operations and marketing can enhance collaboration and bonding through team projects, shared lexicon and mutual task accomplishment. The point is not to get an "A," but to learn how colleagues think and what they like and don't like. Doesn't this resonate as an ideal way for much needed team bonding? Such coordinated training doesn't come cheap but the cost pales in comparison to recruiting a new employee – A new hire costs hundreds of thousands when we are considering the data-intensive digital transformation responsibilities we are aiming for. How much are we willing to spend training a dozen team members? We may still hire from outside the organization but now our existing employees have the knowledge and confidence to integrate approaches from both new and existing people. It's a win–win.

Preference for hiring and leveraging your own comes through loud and clear in our interviews as well. Many of our contacts emphasize the need for retraining and upskilling the existing members of the organization. Even when an outside change agency is involved one of their primary responsibilities should be to focus on internal skill development. For instance, Dr Wang now leads a large digital progress team in Microsoft after having vast experience with transformations during his time in McKinsey. In the interview, he accentuated that throughout the efforts in digital transformation, it is essential to "bring the existing team with you and prepare them to take over when you are gone."

CROSS-DISCIPLINARY

It is clear that many types of teams benefit from having members with non-overlapping points of view. From product development to sports teams, a range of skillsets and biases, even if individually sub-optimal, can combine to yield a result far greater than the sum of its parts. The – now conventional – wisdom in organizational change practice is to bring representatives of various departments and various hierarchical levels into the change management team. The hope here is to make sure the planned change activities are vetted by each of these people at the discussion stage, in order to minimize any glitches in implementation. What we are suggesting here, however, goes a step beyond this approach: Seek out individuals who are trained in different disciplines.

Having a background in different disciplines contributes to the abilities of sensemaking. Sensemaking can be defined as the process we go through as we try to give meaning to the events happening within the organization.[2] This helps define our actions and reactions. As our ability of sensemaking improves, so does our decision quality. Imagine you are in a pitch-black room and you are trying to find your way out. You will start using your senses other than sight and orient yourself through touch, scent or sound. You will try and make sense of the situation as best as you can! The more you can practice using all your senses, the better you will get. In an unexpected business situation, we all try to gather as much information as we can using our various perceptual and intellectual abilities. One of the ways to improve these abilities is to have a varied knowledge base[3] (i.e., having been exposed to and learning about different fields of knowledge). Such a background also makes team members open to learning and have a growth mindset.

A team's ability to see beyond a single discipline can come from several places. While combining people from different disciplines is advantageous, those that have switched domains during their careers also encapsulate the idea of multiple perspectives within a single person. We found effective data communicators and executives started in widely varying backgrounds, from architecture to economics to English literature, who later found their calling in data-centric roles across software engineering, governance and strategy. Within the digital enterprise team at Victoria's Secret, incorporating multiple business backgrounds across retail, operations and finance helps align recommendations and make them more likely to be actionable early on in the insight generation phase, demonstrating the utility of even sub-domain integration.

One should not be shy in hiring across industries as much as disciplines. As Jon Hay of the Red Sox puts it: "We can cherry-pick a lot of the things that other industries are doing well and try and apply those things to our own business." A seemingly familiar job role in one industry may bring entirely different insights in another sector.

Professions, by nature, are conservative and gravitate toward reinforcement rather than change. Across both creative and technological professions such as architecture and IT, we are creatures of habit acculturated with similar educations and indoctrination rituals. These repeated patterns manifest in different ways, from pulling all-nighters to pushing software and hardware updates on the unwilling. Yet, there are ready tools to overcome these challenges. Exposure to "design thinking," for instance, helps integrate understanding of diverse user-centric patterns. As another example, choosing technology platforms that empower the user to experiment rather than merely learn new passwords and protocols places the user in the spotlight from the beginning. When digital transformation recognizes from the very start that the effort, tool or policy will impact people from different backgrounds, measures to account for divergent interpretations and co-creation can be built in from the outset. Along this way, the dashboard can ask the user questions about intended use and provide guidance before generating aggregated charts that may obscure rather than reveal the meaning of specific datapoints, and decisions to pursue. This approach would help change be inclusive from an early stage rather than top-down or from a mono-functional group.

KEY POSITIONS IN ORGANIZATIONAL NETWORKS

The positions people hold in organizational networks impact the speed and ease that a digital transformation can be implemented. As we mentioned, successful digital transformation requires a mindset shift. We have ample evidence in social sciences that a mindset shift through an interpersonal interaction is deemed a "complex contagion."[4] Complex contagion is a process we go through where a behavioral change only takes place if the person is exposed to the idea from multiple sources in their network over a longer period of time. In contrast, simple contagion happens when the two people meet once (e.g., common cold virus and office rumors). Behavioral and cultural changes require complex contagion mechanism to take hold. If the members of the transformation team happen to be in network positions where they have easy and frequent contact with a great number of people, they will be at an advantage in spreading their message.

Network science helps us figure out what these key positions are. Using organizational network analysis, we can figure out the trust and advice networks. Through visual and quantitative analysis of these networks we can tell which individuals would have the highest opportunity to achieve enough influence to secure behavioral change. Put simply, individuals who are central to dense sub-networks (Fig. 5.2, Person A) or who reside in paths that connect multiple sub-networks (Fig. 5.2, Person B) would be the ideal candidates for including in our digital transformation team.

"I-shaped" skills describe people with deep expertise in a single domain. "T-shaped" skills are people who have deep expertise in a domain and also knowledge across multiple domains. In digital transformation, we often see I-shaped profiles manifest as an emphasis on data-centric skills as a way of enhancing an organization's ability to analyze data.[5] However, this can be limiting, as Chief Data and Innovation Officer Jit Kee Chin observes:

> *What's been challenging is finding data professionals that have three essential characteristics: the ability to use the advanced tools, strong business acumen and knowledge of what truly matters, and a deep curiosity to understand what the numbers are telling us.*

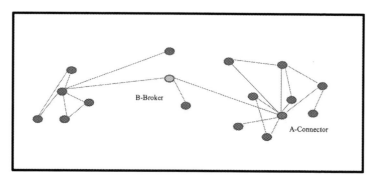

Fig. 5.2. T and I-shaped Skills.

Expanding consideration to T-shaped people can help us increase the chance insights are relevant to the business and discover novel approaches to interpreting seemingly standard analytics output. These T-shaped members have experience thinking from multiple disciplines and if resident in the organization for some time, also the ability to think from the perspective of multiple organizational stakeholders. Here T-shaped refers not only to crossing disciplinary viewpoints, but also the ability to see across functions, departments and hierarchies. Is the ideal hire a person from within the company that has worked across functions and changed career disciplines? Perhaps, but we are aiming to transform the organization to be natively digital and it may even be more desirable to combine team members who are more I-shaped with T-shaped people to help technical expertise more effectively be applied to projects that yield actionable insight.

By reaching more areas of the organization early on, integrating this feedback and communicating more understandably, a recently graduated data engineer, an operations leader and a seasoned exiting project manager can together achieve more transformation than a team of data scientists, engineers and analysts. This cross-disciplinary team consisting of new and existing team members can iterate not only a machine learning model, but also iterate the overall approach to gathering input from organizational members and providing resultant insights to simultaneously refine the digital transformation effort. As data literacy expert Rahul Bhargava succinctly states: "... the earlier you can start iterating on that cycle, the better off you are."

MERGING TECHNICAL AND BUSINESS SKILLS IN DIGITAL TRANSFORMATION

Combining technical and business specialists in the team is key to digital transformation success, but far from easy. Often, it appears that data scientists and business owners live in different worlds. Data scientists sometimes miss the sense of urgency that often drives business people. Business managers are continuously under time pressure caused by needed reactions to competitors and customers. Also, the business group needs to be flexible and able to easily reshape, modify and refine its decisions. Otherwise, it will fail to catch up with the outside world and deliver value to its consumers. Data scientists, however, think long-term rather than "right now" and "today." It aims to deliver solutions that will not work only today, but that will be able to handle a higher demand of tomorrow. That is why many data science solutions often take much longer to implement than those suggested by business people with "need it now" mentality. While the business group considers them as uncooperative, data scientists see most business managers as impatient and shortsighted as they do not allow the data science team to lay the necessary foundation to ensure a system's long-term success.

As a result of this fundamental mindset difference, bringing data scientists and business owners together requires effective communication between them. We offer the following guiding principles to aid this communication:

- *The digital transformation team, especially the data scientists, should know their customers, both internal and external.* As to internal, they should regularly communicate with business clients to learn about their concerns and ways of thinking. How does the company make its money (see Chapter 2)? What are the key opportunities and risks, especially regarding the relationship with customers? As to external, nothing beats hearing the customers themselves talking about their pain points and desires for an even better product or service. This kind of direct engagement creates the urgency and motivation needed for undertaking transformation in a very visceral sense.

- *Data scientists should not be isolated.* Very often, the data science or marketing science department functions as an isolated unit within the organization. It has a different reporting structure and incentive system. It even possesses its own culture, to be more precise, sub-culture: jargon, dress code and work schedule. In our experience, this may please the data scientists in the short run, as they are happily talking to like-minded spirits, but frustrate them in the long run, as business owners don't implement their wonderful tools. Instead, data scientists that sit side by side with their business counterparts enjoy a much healthier and more productive relationship, leading to a larger customer and organizational impact. It is sometimes tough, but always a learning experience to work toward a common goal with colleagues from different backgrounds.

- *Data scientists should understand the firm's business strategy.* It is very important to ensure that there is a common understanding of the business strategy by data scientists and other functional units. This also means that data scientists should be included in the formation of the overarching business strategy. An organization may have multiple objectives, such as cutting costs, expanding overseas and improving customer services. However, these objectives need to be prioritized, which requires assessing a number of trade-offs. The strategy feedback of data scientists should go beyond commenting on whether a desired customer journey or strategy change is technically feasible. For example, McKinsey[6] describes a fast-moving consumer goods company where data scientists create heat maps of potential sources of value creation throughout the company's full business system. This helps business managers understand the relative benefits and costs and make smart trade-offs.

KEY TAKEAWAYS

Choose candidates who have:

(1) demonstrated interest in digital transformation (shows desire to be current and improve);

(2) effective cross-functional communication skills (champion change by influencing others);

(3) connector or broker roles in established trust and advice networks;

(4) cultivated a T-shaped skillset (can champion change by influ-
     encing others); and
(5) an open mind that can adopt an experimental approach.

NOTES

1. The book (by Lewis, M. (2004). *Moneyball: The art of winning
an unfair game*. W. W. Norton & Company) details how the Oakland
Athletics baseball team realized they could recruit combinations of
players who, while individually did not have the most outstanding
player metrics, collectively outperformed in games compared to hiring
players who had the highest metrics. More importantly, it was affordable.
Ironically, they used advanced data analysis to achieve this.

2. Weick, K. E. (1995). *Sensemaking in organizations* (Vol. 3). Sage.

3. Lüscher, L. S., & Lewis, M. W. (2008). Organizational change and
managerial sensemaking: Working through paradox. *Academy of
Management Journal, 51*(2), 221–240.

4. Karsai, M., Iniguez, G., Kaski, K., & Kertesz, J. (2014). Complex
contagion process in spreading of online innovation. *Journal of the Royal
Society Interface, 11*(101), 20140694.

5. Demirkan, H., & Spohrer, J. C. (2018). Commentary—Cultivating
T-shaped professionals in the era of digital transformation. *Service
Science, 10*(1), 98–109.

6. Florian B., Breuer, P., & Suruliz, N. (2014, Summer). Insight-driven
sales transformation. *McKinsey Insights*. https://www.mckinsey.com/
business-functions/marketing-and-sales/our-insight
s/how-leading-retailers-turn-insights-into-profits

6

DESIGN THE OPEN-FLOOR PLAN

Now that we know how to recruit and train the talent to "wield the sledgehammer" of making digital transformation happen, how do we design for it to become ingrained in our organizational culture? In our nested adaptive cycles framework, you can think of culture as the oil lubricating the wheels to work together and binding them as one. Our CEO in New York asked us lots of questions, but an important one we had to ask him was: What is your existing organizational culture, and how do you plan to (re)design it to make digital transformation stick? Believe it or not, the story we told him next concerned blue beings.

Despite a plethora of subsequent three-dimensional (3D) films, Avatar remains the highest grossing 3D film of all time (and indeed among the highest of all films). How has this remained the case decades after its release? Avatar director James Cameron explains Avatar was designed from the start to be a 3D film, beginning with storyboards that were aware of the planned immersive 3D ambience. Every camera angle and digital effect from start to finish reflected this desire for a seamless 3D viewing experience. By the time shooting started, the use of specialized stereoscopic cameras was merely the end result of extensive planning that unequivocally prioritized the viewer. Other films have relied heavily on post-production to achieve a 3D effect, resulting in a compromised experience – to the point where the degree of immersion can vary from terrible to great within a single sitting. The end result is a dissatisfied viewer who leaves disappointed even if they are not consciously aware of the reason for a lackluster movie viewing. Digital transformation in an organization is like making a 3D film, the hypothetical "crowd" (in this case customers and employees) must guide the process from start to finish. It is imperative that digital transformation starts at the very beginning and each step thereafter must be taken with the impacted people and goals in mind.

In our journey through the book, we've talked about goals, gaps and finding the right people to wield the sledgehammer. But how do we infuse both the change process and the end result with a mindset that prioritizes use of technology and information? Getting people to adapt is hard to do – never mind encouraging an entire organization to adopt a digital transformation mindset and implement a collection of digital tools to aid their decision making. Interview after interview illustrates this challenge for industries ranging from apparel (e.g., TJX and Victoria's Secret) to banking, to retail and sports (e.g., Wayfair and the Boston Red Sox). In our consultancy and research experience, we find managers are familiar with the general advice on how to enact change (from excellent books and exercises available on this topic). However, change in regard to digital transformation appears to have several unique features.

Digital transformation is not the adoption of technology but rather the recognition that sustained competitiveness requires native familiarity with data-centric insights. In this sense, digital transformation resembles any other new organizational capability except it can be more aptly viewed as a cultural value rather than a set of specific tasks or processes. The managers we interviewed made this clear when comparing organizations who did (e.g., ServiceNow, Victoria's Secret and Wayfair) versus who did not (yet) have this cultural mindset. It is clear that there are companies who say they're data-driven, but they just use data to confirm the decision they've already made. This can be incredibly frustrating for valuable talent who will inevitably seek alternative places to fulfill their potential. Moreover, professionals may blindly accept an algorithm without realizing its recommendations may be unwise. Cansu Canca observes:

The main assumption appeared to be: the algorithm is mathematical, so it must be right; or if it is robotic, it must be precise. Which is not always the case.

Such hasty adoption happens even in the most sophisticated industries including health care and biotechnology.

Open is the one keyword to remember if you want to understand how to manage your organization's culture to achieve digitalization. In line with our idea of breaking the walls and democratizing data use, digital transformation works best if the firm establishes an *open technology, open culture and open process approach*.[1]

Recognizing this overall perspective makes for a clearer approach to kneading digital transformation in the company culture. As we usually don't have the luxury of forming an organization from scratch, the first step is always determining the existing culture. Identifying the nature of an organization's cultural setting is a valuable step in digital transformation. Just as no shade of blue is better than another, no one culture type is preferable and there may even be a mix of culture types within one area. Nevertheless, once we know the subtleties of our current values, we can figure out the levers to pull for spreading desired values.

TYPES OF ORGANIZATIONAL CULTURE

Yes, all organizations are unique with different industry norms (think of the defense industry with military clients vs the gaming industry), dominant professional formation (think of organizations dominated by lawyers or engineers) and founding histories. However, we want to take a systematic look at multiple companies and benefit from models developed by organizational culture experts. One such model that found a lot of acceptance in the business world is the "competing values framework."[2] This framework assesses the culture based on two dimensions: level of adaptability and locus of focus. The first dimension, level of adaptability, looks at the comfort level with ambiguity. In some organizations, people enjoy the comfort that comes with the presence of well-determined rules. They have formalized processes and predetermined procedures to help guide everyday activities.

There may even be provisions on how to deal with crises. By contrast, other organizations set a limited number of guiding principles and encourage members to use their own judgment and discretion in applying them. The second dimension, locus of focus, looks at where the organization chooses to direct their attention foremost: internal workings and integration of all its departments or external success and differentiating themselves in the markets they operate. Based on these two dimensions, the competing values framework classifies corporate cultures into four main types: clan, adhocracy, hierarchy and market (Fig. 6.1).

Clan cultures, such as Zappos, Tom's of Maine or the Boston Red Sox, combine flexibility with a high internal focus. Such organizations feel like a family, with common purpose, friendly collaboration and strong loyalty bonds. At the Red Sox, a passion for baseball is a common denominator whether you are an athlete, manager or data scientist. When double-headers place incredible demands on cleaning staff, the front office – including managers and data scientists – chip in to help get the stands ready for the next game. These same data scientists present quantitative insights on seat revenue and hotdog prices, while also cleaning alongside

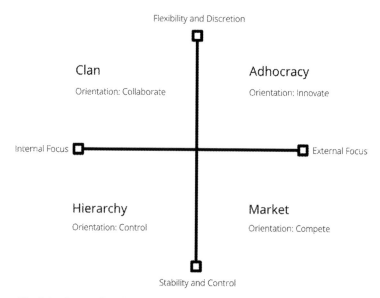

Fig. 6.1. Competing Values Framework.

janitors and managers. The communication of insights derived from machine learning models is therefore received by an audience that is connected to the messenger in a multitude of ways.

A hierarchy is a more traditional culture of internal focus and control to achieve efficiency. These cultures tend to take hold in organizations that compete on cost and/or standardization. McDonald's, and most other fast-food corporations, fall into this category. Process and procedure in day-to-day operations are key, and leaders monitor to keep costs down and ensure rules are followed. Sectors where quality is paramount are also commonly hierarchical because unforeseen complications have a high cost. Construction and the defense industry are typical examples.

Combining external positioning with control, a market culture focuses on results in a competitive environment among colleagues, as is common among investment banking and trading firms. Other prominent examples include Tesla, Amazon and General Electric,[3] with their intense focus on customers combined with formalization in all aspects of their daily operations. In contrast, in adhocracies such as Wikipedia and Google, we observe flexibility along with external focus. In this dynamic and innovative environment, leaders are role models for employees as inspirational innovators willing to challenge assumptions and take chances. Creative groups are often adhocracy-based, such as architecture firms and skunkworks departments. During digital transformation, knowing how to relate quantitative viewpoints with qualitative perspectives is crucial. For example, in architecture, the increasing value realized in interdisciplinary exposure and design-thinking provides a valuable way for data scientists to emphasize the benefits of advanced analytical approaches to urban change. By building a data science function that understood both data and aesthetic design, the architecture firm Arrowstreet was able to assume a pioneering role due to its foresight in proactively providing relatable data-centric insights to clients.

Some organizations also combine elements of two different cultural archetypes. Victoria's Secret, for instance, combines adhocracy culture in adoption of innovative practices, with a market-based culture focused on serving the customer. This facilitates trying new approaches across multiple contexts such as brick and mortar versus online storefronts.

CULTURE – TRANSFORMATION MATCH-UP

As you were reading, you likely thought some of these types of cultures fit with digital transformation ideas more naturally than others. The idea of flexibility, for instance, seems essential in implementing an experimentation approach to making decisions. Emphasis placed on being responsive to market needs is also a push toward use of technologies and information as a fundamental tool in business processes. So adhocracy, with its drive for innovation and main focus on creativity is conducive to digital transformation. Indeed, a recent survey of financial institutions revealed that the conditions that support successful digital transformation are team-based structure, learning through trial error, encouragement of risk-taking and continuous employee training.[4] These conditions are very much in line with norms and values of an adhocracy culture. We might expect the organizations which have an adhocracy culture to have an easier time implementing digital transformation.

Naturally, slowly transitioning into an adhocracy model might be a scenario to consider for those firms that have other kinds of organizational cultures. The choice to go this route should depend on how far the current culture is from a fully flexible, empowered and externally focused culture. If the leap is not drastic, this might be the best course of action. However, we would like to reassure organizations that sport a strong clan, market and even hierarchy culture that there are steps you can take to secure a successful digital transformation.

If your organization fits into a *market culture*, with strong focus on outside competitive forces and desire to control your daily reactions to the markets, you can lean into the market response idea but take it from a performance-focused perspective to an innovation-focused approach.[5] In market organizations, marketing and sales departments tend to hold power and dictate some of the interdepartmental interactions. When we are trying to convince members of this firm to take risks and innovate, we can emphasize the importance of digital tools in responding to customer needs but solicit novel ideas in terms of how they can be integrated into our existing decision systems. The practice of holding on to one aspect of culture while changing other parts can be called "anchoring."

This is one of the tools in use to increase psychological safety and help with transitional periods. Market culture tends to adapt to digital transformation rather well, as long as change agents build on the ability to better satisfy performance metrics when digitalization is achieved.

If you are enjoying a *clan culture* style with strong loyalty bonds and high commitment to the organization, the value to build on is high trust to employees. Relying on this trust, we can ask the transformation team to advocate for digital tools in aiding employees' already strong sense of empowerment. We need to reiterate that openness of data and processes is absolutely key in the clan culture. Any hesitation on the organization's part will create feelings of hypocrisy and mistrust.

The *hierarchy culture* sits at the opposite corner from adhocracy. As such, you might worry that the implementation of digital transformation is hard in such organizations. Although there is some truth to this sentiment, the good news is that we can build on the formalization and codified systems in a hierarchy culture. Strong reasoning and detailed plans backing up the transformation efforts enable members of the organization to shift. That's because the hierarchy culture has established command structures and deep respect for processes and procedures – if you can build digital transformation using these processes and procedures, digital transformation will take hold.

Four general aspects or "levers" can be used to enhance effective change.[6] These levers are:

- *Clarifying meaning*: Set expectations to identify what will and won't change. As mentioned earlier, having an anchor increases the feeling of safety and helps orient the change efforts.

- *Craft milestones*: Assess progress and guide adjustments using clear, time-based milestones. Celebration of these small wins creates momentum and preserves engagement of employees.

- *Communication and symbols*: Explain the "why" as well as the "what." Because we have a variety of mental schemas, what we understand from an identical communication piece might differ drastically. When change agents are using communication medium and different symbols, they should be aware of this fact. Using multiple mediums and exuberant amount of details is one way to combat this. In other words, overcommunicate.

- *Leadership development*: Encourage idea ownership and leading by example. Leaders – both formal and network-based – are seen as role models in periods of transition. Ensuring they are aware of this responsibility and represent all aspects of the change process is important.

KEY TAKEAWAYS

(1) Determine your existing corporate culture.
(2) Understand how your current culture helps versus hinders digital transformation.
(3) Assess the difference between current cultural values and values that help with digital transformation, namely: team-based structure, learning through trial error, encouragement of risk-taking and continuous employee training.
(4) Bridge the gap between current culture and fully digital cultural values.

NOTES

1. Whitehurst, J. (2021). *Organize for innovation*. Red Hat.

2. Adapted from Cameron, K. S., & Quinn, R. E. (2011). *Diagnosing and changing organizational culture: Based on the competing values framework* (3rd ed.). Jossey-Bass.

3. https://www.aihr.com/blog/types-of-organizational-culture/

4. Al-Faihani, M., & Al-Alawi, A. I. (2020). A literature review of organizational cultural drivers affecting the digital transformation of the banking sector. In *2020 International conference on data analytics for business and industry: Way towards a sustainable economy (ICDABI)*. IEEE.

5. Rutihinda, C. (2019). Digital transformation and organizational culture of small and medium size enterprises. *Archives of Business Research*, 7(8), 282–288.

6. For more comprehensive example see Cameron, K. (2008). A process for changing organizational culture. In T. G. Cummings (Ed.), *Handbook of organization development* (pp. 429–445). Sage Publications (Chapter 23).

7

IMPLEMENT TO AVOID THE PITFALLS

Congratulations on making it this far! You've developed the vision for digital transformation (Chapter 2), identified your goals (Chapter 3), used the value chain to identify key gaps (Chapter 4), assembled the dream team (Chapter 5) and leveraged your organizational culture to bridge the gap between current culture and fully digital cultural values (Chapter 6). Now all that is left is successfully implementing digital transformation and learning from mistakes, also from others who shared their experiences with us. In the end, our New York CEO was most interested in this aspect of our advice, telling us: "The devil is in the details!" Yes, we agreed, and also in broad and sustained involvement throughout his organization. Showing our nested adaptation cycle framework, we need to dive deep into the roles of business experimentation, IT and top management support.

Digital transformation clearly needs broad involvement. Successful efforts always include engaging three vital areas of the organization:

- Continuous improvement through experimentation,

- Information technology (IT).

- Managerial support.

CONTINUOUS IMPROVEMENT THROUGH
EXPERIMENTATION

The most important change needed in an organization is one of experimentation or what Williams-Sonoma calls the "create, test, prove, roll" culture. Traditional project management is production-oriented in how it emphasizes set specifications, risk minimization and planning. In contrast, a digitally transformed organization requires managers to have a bias toward execution, with the expectation that plans will change. This expectation stems from inherent uncertainties in the technology and quantitative models required. Why the experimental approach? Because in a digitally transformed organization, the results of actions can be measured very quickly.[1] While, in the past, an alpha or beta product launch may have been needed to gather large-scale data, it is now often possible to create smaller steps in development that generate meaningful data that guide later steps in development:

- As a first example: should the automobile have real-time monitoring of engine health? You can design an experiment where half of people are primed to think they have real-time monitoring and compare their impressions with the control group. The result can be used to guide adjustment of monitoring frequency and privacy limitations.

- As a second example: should we mandate recycling company-wide? You can run an experiment in which you would replace disposable cups with ceramic mugs in one of the company coffee rooms, and compare the opinions of those working close to that room with the rest of the company (control group). The results could also inform how best to communicate the objective and the likely extent of acceptance.[2]

Analytics dashboards (where outputs change with the user changing inputs[3]) play a key role in helping adopt an experimentation culture as they allow managers to "experiment" by adjusting inputs and monitoring the forecasted output before committing resources. Such systems could be constructed internally, or you may partner with one of the many digital platforms available today that can streamline and optimize continuous experimentation (such as Optimizely).

LEVERS TO PULL WHEN ENABLING EXPERIMENTATION

Adhocracy cultures adopt experimentation without any need for encouragement. Market cultures respond to milestones in the form of incentives. It is particularly important to emphasize clarity in hierarchical-type firms and leadership tends to play a larger role in both clan and hierarchy cultures.

METRICS AND IT

Continuous improvement via experimentation is only possible if the risk of each experiment is low and the results can be quickly and accurately assessed. Therefore, frequently collected and widely available data are essential to a digitally transformed organization. In marketing, information is so crucial that Chief Information Officer (CIO) and Chief Marketing Officer (CMO) often receive joint reports. Importantly, every experiment should measurably relate to a process that can be improved. Each experiment should have outcomes that can be acted upon for the next action or experiment.

The first step for any firm that desires to truly digitally transform is to implement firm-wide IT infrastructure capable of not only unifying data, but also generating key metrics that can be used to assess progress. At Wayfair, top management realized that there were too many key performance metrics that impeded efforts to drive digital change. Worse still, different performance metrics were often referred to by the same name. An organization-wide effort was made to standardize key performance metrics which allowed each department and function to share a common goal and meaningfully track performance over time. The next step is to adopt a platform enabling fast dissemination of experimental results. 7-Eleven, Procter and Gamble and Williams-Sonoma all took this first step.

This is similar to what Davenport and Harris[4] call stage 4: "Enterprise-wide analytics capability under development." Without a centralized information repository and widespread accessibility of information including key progress metrics, democratic adoption of digital transformation is severely impeded as people lose track of project progress and thus the ability to prioritize.

Accessibility means both availability and interpretability. It is no use sharing highly technical data that cannot be understood by decision makers. We found organizations often defer to business intelligence (BI) tools to provide standardized dashboards, yet these representations are typically generated without due consideration of the audience or the decisions that will be made. A standard dashboard often includes legacy tables and graphs that take up valuable real estate on the screen and distract from the problem at hand. Next time you see a dashboard, think to yourself:

> *Is this dashboard showing me default aggregate output that includes irrelevant historical data and averages across regions and/or marketing channels? Is this drowning out new edge cases capable of hinting at early problems or opportunities?*

Care must be taken to engage a design-thinking approach to help develop a reporting system that reveals rather than obfuscates data-based insights. As one senior data scientist told us: "People do not know what they should be looking for; they have tons of dashboards shared but don't know where to start."

It is impossible to collate data and generate meaningful metrics in hierarchical cultures without *explicit* and *formal* IT integration. The physical infrastructure of hierarchical firms reflects a tendency for managerial inertia and therefore the physical systems must change in conjunction with cultural norms. Proctor and Gamble created a whole new global unit for IT services that enabled functionality and, even more crucially, also communicated and clarified to managers this explicit cultural shift. The "why" and the "what" were made very clear.

Organizational stakeholders are often skeptical when large-scale changes in infrastructure are announced and functions are asked to work more closely together. Moreover, by virtue of its traditional mandate to preserve system integrity and standardize practices to reduce risk, IT is not a natural driver of digital transformation. Therefore, it is especially important make sure that IT serves as a critical enabler of digital transformation, rather than submits to being a mere expansion of a support unit in the value chain.

LEVERS TO PULL WHEN ENGAGING IT

By giving IT a stake in digital transformation *milestones*, members within IT are able to better appreciate that they are an integral part of analytics rather than a mere data provider and can therefore encourage rather than resist change. Collaboration among the CIO, the Chief Technology Officer and the CMO can further send *clear leadership signals* that functions should collaborate rather than merely "support" one another.

MANAGERIAL SUPPORT

Managerial leadership is key to any successful change, including digital transformation. When team members have the backing of their managers, they feel empowered to suggest alternatives and challenge the status quo. Otherwise, the default is to take requests from internal clients and the game of "picking the projects based on likely political repercussions" ensues. For instance, Meredith Machovoe of Service Now says: "I'm lucky that every project I work on has a direct link to company operations/actions." This is enabled by a flat hierarchy where top management meets at least weekly with the insights team. This investment pays great dividends in the long run. After continually integrating input from management over time at the Red Sox, Jon Hay highlighted the benefit of engaging management: "… where we are good is internal capital. We are at the point where almost every team we work with has a lot of trust."

LEVERS TO PULL WHEN SECURING MANAGERIAL SUPPORT

In our experience and that of our interviewees, we have identified these three key levers we recommend you pull for managerial support:

(1) Provide clear expectations and incentives, but also ensure there are tangible milestones and reward metrics.
(2) Redefine return on investment to include insight generation from decisions, which would reward doing experiments. At the same time, be careful that this doesn't lead to experiments being run for their own sake because that can waste resources on experiments where the answers are largely already known.
(3) Engage managers in experimentation. Start with localized applications that provide incremental insights. As data literacy expert Rahul Bhargava observed: "… the earlier you can start iterating on that cycle, the better off you are."

Managers trust their instinct and experience. They must be given the opportunity to test their judgment against hard metrics to help them combine these two decision-making norms and refute either approach where the data indicate it is justified. Early on in digital transformation, it was rare for senior management to be able to understand which metrics to prioritize. Seemingly effective metrics became perfunctory such as "run 10 experiments per week," which, instead of generating valuable insights as per the original purpose of experiments, just became a way to confirm existing thinking through designing confirmatory studies rather than exploratory trials. The tendency for managers to be risk-averse has to be changed through *communication* of new *incentives* that reward insight generation during the experimentation process as much as overall returns. We advise engaging managers through interactive dashboards and incremental involvement in the experimental process. If buy-in occurs, hierarchical cultures can in fact adopt more quickly due to leadership.

TYING IT ALL TOGETHER: SEVEN PITFALLS IN DIGITAL TRANSFORMATION AND HOW TO AVOID THEM

Implementation is more than the sum of its parts. Even with the ability to engage across organizational cultures and use change levers, there are bound to be bumps along the digital transformation road. Many organizations have tried to digitally transform, and we have learned both from their successes and failures. As our final advice, we discuss seven pitfalls identified by decision makers we interviewed and concrete ways to overcome them:

(1) Treating digital transformation as a goal unto itself.
(2) Moving fast and breaking things.
(3) Increasing expectations while failing to align moving parts.
(4) Overcentralize versus democratize data and tool access.
(5) Failing to prioritize digital transformation across the organization.
(6) Being too cheap to pay for specialized talent.
(7) Becoming obsessed with the shiny new thing.

First, digital transformation runs the risk of becoming a *goal unto itself* rather than a specific and conscious effort to improve an underlying task. This pitfall occurs when the focus is on technology rather than decision making. Instead, the most successful digital transformers focus on usability and how people learn in the organization. As data literacy expert Rahul Bhargava described:

> *In digital transformation the agency is on digital, not on the thing being transformed. But when you integrate something there's two parties. What is the other one in your case? I would encourage you to think about that question because you could have a lot of answers that are all valid, but which one you care about most can guide you into a terminology that better reflects your ideas and what's the thing being transformed.*

Successful organizations know "Technical skills are necessary but not sufficient" and, in order to hit the ball out of the park, "The goal is not to have the best model, the goal is to affect change." Moreover, larger budgets tend to reduce managers' critical eye in questioning the ongoing profitability of the digital transformation effort.

A key recent example is curbside pickup,[5] which has been celebrated as a big deal. Sure, this sounds like a great service, but, in your industry, how many of your customers truly want it? And are they willing to pay for the extra costs of this service in your supply chain? Just as with delivery, you still need an employee to walk up and down the aisle and fill a cart!

How can you avoid this pitfall? By asking "why" and "how" questions, which can be institutionalized as "frequently asked questions" that should become part of every proposal.

Ask follow-ups about:

(1) What are the reasons behind the initiative – how did it start?
(2) What is the timing of the change effort?
(3) Who are involved, is there a change team, who is the owner?
(4) What pain points do you expect in the process?
(5) What impact are you hoping to achieve? What has to happen to make this a reality?

We've heard a great example from Jon Hay (Red Sox), who is very big on the two-by-two matrix (impact by effort) and delivering high impact work at low effort:

> Work on things that can really move the needle in the short term. Try to never go in that bottom left quadrant of low impact-high effort, which I think sometimes, especially in the IT world people get distracted by shiny objects and find that there's a really interesting challenge that will take a long time, but maybe not be that impactful. So, I think that's part of it and then really it's working with stakeholders and saying: "You know everyone, we do have 150 internal customers and everyone's project is the highest priority, right?" Because to them it is absolutely important, I think part of my job as the president in the department was to have those frank conversations: "Here are other things that are coming from people in your department, or adjacent to you. How do we think about what the priority order is? And by the way, how can we maybe align some of these things for more efficiency." For instance, Premium Sales needs an inventory management tool to manage our sweet inventory, but Fenway events is an inventory management tool to manage all of the different days and assets they have. Could we put them on the same timeline, build one massive inventory management tool and deliver that to both customers at the same time?

A second pitfall is best expressed in the slogan "move fast and break things." This outdated tech mantra was always controversial, and simply cannot be applied indiscriminately in today's environment. Lack of diversity in thought processes is a key problem, especially when shortcutting the development and launch process. Several "old-timers" indicated they used to push a great idea live immediately. Today, the launch process has become much more structured as the consequences of launching a bad product can be substantial. This includes not only legal ramifications but also user accessibility, which has come to the forefront in the last couple of years: "More people have accessibility issues online than technology issues. We have strict policies now."

An example of including accessibility is building a vacation rental product. While US employees may have a good idea of how North Americans and Europeans book vacation rentals, they often don't know the practical issues in Latin America and Asia-Pacific. For instance, a US team found that Indonesians were not using credit cards to make bookings and sent a research team to the country to determine why. They found that societal values frown upon taking on debt, and, consequently, most potential customers prefer debit over credit cards. They then adjusted the product for accessibility with prepaid debit cards. Investigations of this type, and continuous small stakes experimentation are the natural antidote to a tendency to move fast and break things.

A third pitfall is that digital transformation problems are becoming increasingly disparate, that is, involving *moving parts from multiple partner teams*. When a partner wants to change something, as they often do, it impacts everything else. One example is video streaming subscriptions, where the partner gives you information in exchange for views. The partner may be initially satisfied but then wants more content. Expectations can increase over time, even if the subscription amount is the same. In the best organizations, digital transformers work across multiple teams to ensure data integrity and consistency.

As Nate Nichols highlights:

> *Sometimes people do not know what they should be looking for, they have tons of dashboards shared but don't*

know where to start. They are not clear on which dash-
board or tool should be used. They've got three BI tools,
one of them has 80% of the data, the other one has 15%
of that data and the other one has 10% with different
overlaps. Data needs to get filtered and sorted to where it
is coming from, the trust issues around the data need to
be solved.

As a recent case study, an architecture firm had to rapidly transform in the wake of the pandemic. When the data science function
was started in 2017, the question used to be:

"What does it look like to have a data science function in
an architecture firm?" Over time, clients pushed for more
state-of-the-art solutions, which drove senior leadership
to ask: "How can we make better decisions for the work
that we are doing?"

At the same time, *over-centralization is a common pitfall.* Data
are changing societies and in particular power and participation, so
democratizing this power is key to enable more people to participate. We observe the growth of citizen artificial intelligence developers. In some organizations, 80–90% of data initiatives begin
with the IT department, which is not typically concerned with
change and improved decision making. Our interview with Rahul
Bhargava dug deep into this pitfall:

When I think about power, I think about the ability to
authentically engage and change the circumstances for
oneself or for a community that they're involved in. That
typically for me is trying to democratize rather than cen-
tralize power. If we look at most businesses that have suc-
ceeded in various forms of what one calls digital adoption
or transformation, they often have a combination of top-
down and bottom-up approaches. When you see things
like rich media document editing 30 years ago or smart-
phones, they are two examples that came more from the
bottom-up approach where people brought those tools
into the workplace and the workplace adapted to support
and augment and take partial ownership of those tools to

*the point where you'll see mobile tool adoption from the
top down and you'll see it pushed from the bottom up.*

For instance, in performance dashboards, the typical business
focus is how to measure an employee's or department's performance so that an appropriate reward could be given or punish-
ment assigned. A better way is to use the data to help people do
their job better and further their careers. The book *It's Not the
Size of the Data, It's How You Use It* gives concrete tips on how
to gain employee buy-in, including involving them in the project
from the start, giving them specific levers to pull to improve their
performance and running a trial to find and steam out wrinkles in
the dashboard design.

More recent approaches at data democratization include a giant
screen in the same room for shared ownership, as a mirror of "us"
not a "window" into somewhere else:

> *I like things where you have a giant screen in the same
> room where a lot of people are working on the same thing
> being represented on the screen. So, there's like a shared
> ownership of what feels like a mirror for us and not a win-
> dow of somebody looking down at us from outside. That
> mirror is an example of a version that creates a very dif-
> ferent narrative. If we're seeing all of our work up there,
> then there's a sense of shared ownership that could be cul-
> tivated. So sometimes there's like social changes that are
> very small that work within business language and struc-
> ture and then having something that talks about that not
> in a punitive way, but like, oh okay, here's a trend we're
> seeing, help me understand this trend. But not here's a
> trend we're seeing you need to work harder on. So much
> of it is just social.*

A fourth pitfall is *unaligned priorities for digital in the organization.* Leadership signals lack of priority by delegating digital transformation and only sporadically checking up. Instead, leaders in
the most successful organizations have regular meetings with owners of digital transformation. Several interviewees left their initial
company because leadership stated digital will never be a priority.

Instead, they landed at organizations where digital drives the business, while brick-and-mortar locations support digital. Key examples include Apple, Victoria's Secret and Amazon's flagship stores.

This does not mean, however, that predigital companies can't successfully transform – it does mean that they need to pay special attention to aligned priorities throughout the organization. For instance, National Geographic (Nat Geo) changed its full tech stack to allow better consumer interactions (*IT*), upgraded its website from "great for marketing" to also "great for Search Engine Optimization" (*web developers*), reminded its *content and graphics teams* that they should not just write and think about the iconic print version *and* discovered that customers still want said print version even in the app (*app development teams*). Culture eats technology for breakfast: the key to digital transformation is changing how people think and work together. For instance, foldout maps and infographics look awesome in print, but how to leverage content in audio, podcasts, short videos that feature Q&A with the hero being highlighted? Moreover, Nat Geo knows it is not the go-to site for breaking news, but instead aims to be the go-to site for the "double click" – for example, explaining how borders have grown historically with insightful maps. Again, this requires alignment of priorities for this digital vision.

Likewise, leadership in successful organizations addresses *ethical issues* head on. Originally, ethical issues were raised grassroots, by employees, but have not been top priority to leadership, who often assumes that "because it is the output of a model, it must be correct and precise." Nowadays ethical issues are at the forefront because leadership does not want to embarrass the company and lose customers. We advise leaders to discuss the ethical components from the start and put in place dedicated plans and teams. As Cansu Canca offered:

> *I think now, finally, organizations/companies are realizing that there are ethical issues and they have to deal with them, preferably from the beginning. But I can still not say that they are doing it right. I think the good part is that now there's more awareness. They are putting in place dedicated teams, so that is a big plus. Previously it*

was only grassroots, and that didn't go anywhere because the leadership was not interested. Now, there is an interest from the leadership and there's grassroots interest. And they are trying. I mean, I think both of these aspects, both the leadership and the grassroots are coming together.

For instance, Microsoft has created a structure where ethics teams are more connected with intermediaries who can escalate issues from different roles. This is an improvement from just having stand-alone ethics teams, which acted more like internal review boards. The old structure saw ethical issues discussed grassroots in an innovation team, but without creating any relevant documentation or reflecting back on these issues after the product was launched. In the new structure, ethics intermediaries actively go out to innovation teams to talk about what the issues are, what they would do about it and how it connects across the organization.

Lack of specialization and willingness to pay for specialized talent is a key pitfall mentioned by our interviewees. While data transformation initially started with a "jack of all trades," companies now have specific needs for which they need to pay market salaries. The Chief Financial Officer need not fully understand the details, but needs to enable and give trusted people the tools they need. In this respect, digitally born firms have less "tech debt," while leaders and teams at other organizations would often seek data to confirm existing thoughts instead of being truly data-driven.

A key example comes from our interviewee contemplating changes in hiring over the last five years:

It was easier to find that Jack of all trades, because we had so many holes to fill. I could bring in someone that wasn't necessarily a data scientist, but was a hardcore statistician. But to do a lot of things well, they could learn new things and could communicate well, a little bit more of a "five tool player." Now I feel when I'm hiring, I'm filling a very specific need because we want to build out the department. I'm looking for someone that can do a very specific thing very well and that's where it starts to get tricky. We just recently hired an analyst on our team and for the first time we had a hard time at the end to convince people. Our industry doesn't always pay well but had some perks, which have become less valuable with the pandemic. Now you're competing for technical talent that knows what they're worth, and they can go to literally anywhere, regardless of location. It's actually been an effort for us to convince our senior executives – "Hey look, if you want these sorts of people, to hire data architects you gotta pay market rate."

Finally, don't become *obsessed with the shiny new thing*, believing it will replace all others. Several technologists criticized Meta for excessively subsidizing the Oculus Quest and making it "too gamey" to be taking seriously in virtual reality (VR) communities. We also heard that "the death of the desktop is not coming, it's never going to happen. VR is not going to replace the desktop, VR is going to augment the desktop." Likewise, the development team at National Geographic had ensured that the layout looked great on a phone screen, but was surprised to learn that customers still wanted a link to the pdf version of the magazine. Improving the user experience resulted in a vast improvement in the app rating, from 1.3 to 4 + stars. We have seen similar stories played out in the newspaper industry; for example, the New York Times installing a paywall but allowing some free articles and keeping its iconic print version, of which the weekend edition is especially appealing to a key section of loyal users. Good old marketing principles remain crucial, from understanding the customers to properly segmenting, targeting and positioning in your marketing strategy.

KEY TAKEAWAYS

(1) Implement within the organizational culture(s) in which you operate.
(2) Determine the levers that will work best in enabling (a) experimentation, (b) IT and (c) gaining managerial support.
(3) Rank the top three pitfalls you expect to encounter and how to avoid each of them.
(4) Repeat the above when a change cycle is encountering problems or completed. What could be adjusted?

THE NEXT STEP!

Interacting with the thoughtful practitioners and practical academics in this book, you and we have grown in our conviction that digital transformation is not just adopting technologies or revising individual tasks. Instead, it is all about the interaction of vision, task and talent throughout the organization. Coming back to our nested adaptation model, it is key to ensure the gears turn together, with the business wheels spinning as fast as the customers change, while IT and top management provide the technical and vision framework in which business can be successful. Just as you wouldn't exercise one muscle to get fit, it's essential to ensure all people and all functions learn how to work together to enhance the overall ability to deliver better solutions for the customer. We aimed to provide an integrative framework based on actual client settings, and combined our academic insights with interviews and examples from leaders across positions and industries.

If you want to take the next step, organizations such as the American Marketing Association can help, both by providing training and insights and by bringing you together with other managers and practical academics. This book grew out of such interactions, which crystallized around "The seven problems of marketing." While this book focuses on the problem of "Managing the digital transformation of the modern corporation," its message is consistent with the other published books in the series. For one, Liam Fahey writes in *The Insight Discipline* that:

- The "big data" juggernaut results in many analysis projects becoming scavenger hunts for data patterns; the report card regarding decision value is mixed at best.

- Bright and capable analysts and analysis teams generate what they consider key findings, but they're unable to discriminate between what's important for the business and what isn't.

We fully agree and hope that our perspective on digital transformation of the full organization, complements Lurie's refinement of what an insight actually is and how to increase your chances of uncovering and using insights. Likewise, in *The Organic Growth Playbook*, Jaworski and Lurie focus on deeply understanding the customer journey to deliver compelling behavior change value propositions, therefore profitably and sustainably growing your business. Our current book shows how to sustain digital transformation in the dynamic nested adaptation model, detailing both top management responsibilities for vision and business responsibilities for using digital tools to reimagine the customer journey map. While *The Organic Growth Playbook* showed you that changing just a few high-yield customer behavior can drive faster revenue growth, we hope to inspire you on how to do so with the new technologies becoming available year after year.

So what are you waiting for? Engage in the digital transformation and let us know what you have learned!

NOTES

1. On why big data does not always mean better decisions but needs to be combined with experimentation as startups do, see: Seggie, S. H., Soyer, E., & Pauwels, K. H. (2017). Combining big data and lean startup methods for business model evolution. *AMS Review, 7*(3), 154–169.

2. We are grateful to the design thinking team at Experience Point for this example.

3. See the definition of Analytic Dashboards in Chapter 1 of Pauwels, K. H. (2014). *It's not the size of the data – It's how you use it: Smarter marketing with analytics and dashboards.* https://www.amazon.com/Its-Not-Size-Data-How/dp/0814433952

4. Davenport, T., & Harris, J. G. (2017). *Competing on analytics, the new science of winning.* Harvard Business Review Press.

5. https://www.nytimes.com/2020/10/09/business/retailers-curbside-pickup.html

8

LEARN FROM THE EXPERIENCES OF OTHERS

In researching this book, we conducted interviews across industries, roles and managerial levels and found incredible insights from established thought leaders to managers in the thick of enacting change. The interviewees represented all the gears in our nested adaptation cycles framework: from Chief Data Officers and Vice Presidents (VPs) to Heads of Business Insights and Data Governance. Some of these interviewees were even so kind as to give us permission to share the full conversation with you. Recognizing how curious minds love deriving their own conclusions from raw data, we present these conversations here. All thoughts are those of individuals and do not represent the views of any organizations with whom they may be affiliated or otherwise.[1] All errors in transcription and editing are our own.

Patrick McQuillan, Head of Data Governance
Jit Kee Chin, Chief Data and Innovation Officer
Rahul Bhargava, Data Literacy Professor
Cansu Canca, Founder and Director, AI Ethics Lab
Jon Hay, Vice President, Data, Intelligence and Analytics
Daniela de Aguiar, Senior Analyst
Neil Hoyne, Chief Measurement Strategist
Meredith Machovoe, Head of Business Insights

David Saffo, Researcher in Computer Science
Tyler Shannon, Senior Design Strategist

PATRICK MCQUILLAN

Head of Data Governance

Interviewer: Could you give us a description of what you do?

Patrick: I first started out in communications last year. I was the Director of Analytics for Allen & Gerritsen, which is New England's largest independent advertising agency. I worked for a media firm, and I was doing mainly marketing work in marketing analytics for our US operations, and I recently transitioned in December 2021 over to Wayfair. I'm spearheading their data governance wing. I'm serving as a lead in their service vertical, so I'm focusing on all service data across the entire organization, North America and Europe for any KPIs we have; essentially understanding how those end users respond to our work, our efforts, what we can do to improve on that, how we can ensure that we're getting positive results over the long term and meeting long term goals set by the execs and senior leadership. The work that I do specifically with data governance is that I manage a team that right now is responsible for two primary functions.

The first function is intuitive based on the title of the role and that is to work across 40 or 50 different teams and vertical groups to make sure that we align on clear definitions of each *KPI* that we're measuring, make sure that everyone has a clear, lateral view of what success means and how it's being defined and understood across different groups, making sure that we're holding those people accountable for reporting that information for any sort of manual or automated querying that they're doing at any sort of back end maintenance. We work closely with the data engineering team to make sure that a lot of that is taken care of and ensure there's strong data integrity.

The second function is basically proving our effectiveness and insight reporting to the executives. This means everything from the junior execs like regional GM's or full scale across a service organization. We have calls with the COO to set targets and set goals for making sure that we have a clear cross-vertical narrative that we can share about how everything is doing, not just within these different lanes but across, and ensure that we can provide a bit more of a strategic recommendation and also to update on how the big picture is doing, and build a narrative around that. So it's our responsibility to summarize and maintain integrity of that data and ensure that it's being passed along in a strategic way that tells a full story to inform decision making.

Interviewer: I'm fascinated by both roles. I've investigated them academically and also with smaller companies. Can you tell me about the biggest challenges and the wins or things that you have learned that could be done better on defining KPIs. If people define the KPI differently then we have no common ground. So you typically have to define it exactly the same and you have to really ensure that but people can show their creativity on how to increase that KPI once it's defined. So how do you get consensus on that when everybody is trying to cherry pick their own definitions and how do you compare things across verticals?

Patrick: In other words, how do we ensure compliance with the KPIs we put forward and how do we ensure that you know that there is a clear definition? It's more of an art than a science, especially in a large organization. Wayfair is 16,000 people and our service organization is about 3,500 people. So we have a lot of different owners for those KPIs. We first try to ensure that everything is based on a consistent plan and understanding. We have a very consistent road map that we're trying to meet. Right now, we're working with our execs to help make sure that they have a clear set of goals that they have outlined to us, and where those are not clear, we seek out those clarifications. Then we make sure that as things continue to change, they change below a very rigid straight line that is dictating those actions, and that's what we always want to revisit. So once we have those clear directives and we know that they are immutable, at least for the coming year or 18 months, then based on that we will reach out and coordinate with these different KPI owners. The main point of struggle is that we have to see if there are multiple duplicates of a KPI. For example, revenue per unit sold. Maybe every different group has a different understanding of what that looks like because it has to fit within their purposes and they're only operating within their circles. So maybe the sales team thinks of it differently than the marketing team. However, because each team will look at revenue from a slightly different formula, they'll look at units under a different breakout, or sales, or compounded aggregated over a different timeframe for different groups. At the end of the day, what we'll do is one of two things. We'll either consolidate them under a single KPI if it makes the most sense to meet that higher level goal or we will break them out and rename them so that they don't follow the same nomenclature, but have their own unique name under unique ownership. That way we can continue telling a story that's more self-explanatory without having to have three of the same things and explain what each of them are. We can call something revenue per unit, and another sales per contact, so it's slightly different based on a uniform definition. That takes a lot of managing over time, especially when you're trying to update the definition of something.

There's also the retroactive update of looking through our previous reports and our databases and saying, now we have to find a way to do this retroactively which can be a struggle if the same cloud was different a year ago versus now. So all that comes into play, but ultimately we just make sure that we have the sign-off before any final initiatives are put into place. The last point I'll add is that it does become complicated where there are teams who just maybe due to the bandwidth are unable to address it. You have these folks who are doing manual pulls, while we do have automated stuff where you can just program it in but there's some teams that just have to update and plug and play and pull something out and update it each week. Due to the nature of how the data are produced, we have to make sure that when we do make these adjustments, we accommodate for that.

Interviewer: For the second function, you have things from social media and you have things from TV and shows, so how do you ensure that's comparable or compatible? For instance, the social media group measures things very differently than the TV group. So, how do you give a more strategic recommendation about what's going on in the total organization?

Patrick: I know it might sound buzzwordy and business-y but I think we know that at the end of the day the only way to secure something that works is to make sure that we're all referring back to the same foundation that drove the initiative in the first place. Storytelling comes into play to prove our effectiveness, and it's really about moving from a week-to-week conversation where, oh this is how it did, and here's the number for that. We talk about the history of what's been happening and provide context around why that trend line isn't moving in the direction we want it to. Step 2 is talking about where we currently are and then comparing the historical trend and why maybe it's higher or lower. And then lastly, we try to fit that into a plan for moving forward. That can be short-term depending on the nature of the metric, maybe there's some grand overarching story behind something like revenue. Our customer service reps and the way they're being rated on the way they're addressing any outstanding issues with delayed orders or returns is more short term. Maybe we just want to look at the past couple of months and just have a plan set for the next month or two and it's just being able to treat each core metric. We have hundreds of

KPIs but looking at these 10 or 15 main ones that senior management really cares about and being able to treat each one as its own, so having a separate story, a different plan for each of them and pretty much giving them their own inheritance of priorities, their own road map for conversation and their own context so that it's not always a three-month plan. Maybe one makes sense for a year, one makes sense for a quarter and having each person who owns that individual KPI giving them the right stage and platform to have that dialogue with the appropriate supporting metrics.

Interviewer: I'm fascinated with the 10–15 main KPIs upper management cares about. What is the process about which that was established? Is it something that came top down that upper management says, hey, you really have to do these things? Is it bottom up that people said, hey, you know this is just very useful to us and we want to own these things? Or is it something that started from that and then over the years or decades grew into it? How did you come up with the 10–15 main ones?

Patrick: Yeah they came from a lot of conversations from before I had joined. As our data infrastructure continues to evolve, we're able to answer those in more nuanced ways. We try not to update them very often. Right now, we're trying to do an update because we're entering the new year, so it's more situational, but we try not to. We try not to schedule a time to update them or make it a regular practice. It's more so where it makes sense and where we're pivoting. So the Chief Executive Officer (CEO) will maybe take a new position or care about something new. That'll trickle down and that'll hit us, and then we'll just say, oh, it makes sense. Overall, we try to keep it consistent, at least for the main KPIs because with the more detailed metrics, those will be more in-depth conversations with more of the immediate managers, or the senior regional managers, but in terms of COO's and CEO's, they'll just want one slide or two with just what's going on for each set of metrics.

Interviewer: How do you see where you stand in terms of what people call a data-driven organization? And how did you get there and what do you think has to fall in place to get even better at it?

Patrick: I think *coordination, organization and alignment* are the big three words. Before I joined Wayfair, the largest organization I ever worked in my entire career was the United Nations. I worked there for about a year and a half and that was a 20,000 person organization. It can become much less organized in larger organizations. But aside from the United Nations, everything I worked in was consulting firms, in which typically the teams are smaller, they're more focused, and it's easier to be organized and easier to get by.

But now that I'm back in that larger organization environment, yes, it's – it's much harder to align and it's much more challenging to be agile. While you are being agile, you are able to institute change, but it can't happen overnight. You have to incrementalize that change over months to make sure that it doesn't ruffle feathers or doesn't shock anybody or it doesn't disrupt the system. So what I would say is the most important component is just ensuring that everything is communicated. You have *the right people and everyone else to sign off on it and filed in triplicate before you can upload.*

Interviewer: Is signing up with the right people the major task of top management like supporting you and signing off? I have a brother who calls his mid-management position as the shaman who interprets what the spirits above say to people down and vice versa. So you get the sign up there and then, what you really need is a buy-in from the rest of the organization.

Patrick: Usually the way it works is that it's a bit of a bounce around. So we have our initial goals that we want to meet. It's about getting that full meeting on board or a couple of full meetings with the folks who are working laterally with me, or with the senior managers who will be reporting to me or other folks in my position and just the people who are close enough to the data but still have a view of the bigger picture. Get that buy-in and get what we need from each other's separate lanes. And then we share that with the senior management and then there will be a digestion period when we'll course correct and then hopefully that only has to happen once, maybe twice, but then at the end of the day depending on the sides of the initiative, we'll get that buy-in. In my experience at least, it has been about one, maintaining the integrity of data which is more internal, secondly, ensuring that it makes sense after the re-alignments and making sure that the past state and future state are equal when you factor out time from the situation.

Interviewer: You've had a career over a lot of time and across domains so are there measures that used to be effective that are not as effective these days in achieving change or concepts in technology and transformation analytics that are no longer the same as they used to be?

Patrick: Updating spreadsheets off of the cloud, for one. I think the most important thing that's beginning to shift now is the fact that senior decision makers like VP's and the C-Suite are finally being forced to understand what data-driven decision making means. I feel like in 2005 or even 2014 there would be instances where you'd have these very high-tech, front leading firms, but most managers didn't come from that data science background. If you graduated college in 2003, odds are by the time it's 2012 you don't really have a background in data science. But for the people who graduated in 2008 when you're managing them there's a bit of disconnect, and so a lot of the way you talk about it, the way you understand it, the way you build initiatives like the need to be

AI driven or data driven, they didn't really know what that meant. A lot of people just thought that there was a period where anything that was machine learning would get VC funding. No one needed to know what it actually was. It could be natural language processing, It could be a neural net, no one knew. Now that field is beginning to mature and it's starting to get into the mid-state where there's not full adoption but there is very rapid adoption that we're starting to see. Managers are now being held more accountable, especially with all this open source like the infrastructure that we have now to actually know what they're talking about. I remember when I started my career, the folks whom I was doing data work for, they would give us a request and want it in 20 minutes and I'd say, well, let me just query this perfect data link like that doesn't exist and get this to you. They didn't understand. Now the folks I work with such as my manager, who is, older than me comes from a data engineering background and he has done that work and that way we're able to have much more productive dialogue, and I'm noticing companies are beginning to hire more and more qualified senior folks to make those decisions.

Interviewer: When you said that in a hypothetical organization, the manager that you reported to didn't come from a data background. Does that mean you used to go bend over backwards to reinterpret the message to fit this schema? Did you not have as much data as you would like?

Patrick: There wasn't very strong data in all of my previous roles. I think the end goal was the same almost all of the time, but two things would be different. One would be understanding how to fully activate the tools that we have at our disposal, like there were so many times where I would introduce a model and it was so easy to impress these guys because maybe they're coming from a more spreadsheet-based background and to them that's data driven. But you started saying, hey, we can automate this and all of a sudden they didn't even know we could do it.

So we're hitting the same points that they want to hit, but they're not quite sure of the full value, we could flesh out from what we currently have on-hand. Secondly, while setting expectations and project management you would have these wild requests where the data teams would always be under a lot of pressure and there'd be a lot of turnover because they're being asked to run these crazy models. Just a week ago a manager said, hey, can we see this number by the end of the week without understanding how the ETL process looks like or understanding what that data link looks like. This is because they don't have that context or that technical background, they're not really quite sure how to time or manage those asks and it creates a lot of downward pressure on the folks on those teams that are starting to disappear. I've been seeing less and less of it over the years. It's still definitely case by case, but I have been seeing less and less of it on average.

Interviewer: This very much reminds me about my start too in the early 2000s. I worked in companies, in the marketing department and when I give them a model I'd get "Yeah, I understand your model, but there's no way I can explain this to my boss or my bosses boss." Nowadays there's people very high up in marketing organizations who really know what they're talking about.

Patrick: Indeed, and I'd like to close with a great story that I think might be helpful. It didn't happen to me, but it happened with a colleague of mine. So I used to work in economic consulting, which if you guys are aware is litigation consulting. There's statistical work and coding and you work exclusively with lawyers. When I was working in Chicago, a colleague of mine, he was a senior analyst at the time, guy from Northwestern, got an ask – we had received over 40,000 documents to review. They were all spreadsheets all in similar formats, and we had to set it up. We would have to take about five months to download all this information and to just stack it, to be able to create a giant unified body and create a giant data set. Most of it was standardized. We were saying it's going to take half a year before we can get started on this and overnight my friend, who had just taught himself Python decided he could write a script that would just download it all overnight. So we're on a call, maybe a couple days in and our boss is freaking out about how we're going to get this all done. So he calls us and he goes "Today you just take files 1 to 50 I'll take 51 to 100. Alex, you take 101 to 150" and Alex goes "Can I actually take 101 to 40,000?" He's like I can do it probably in a couple of days. I'll just let it run overnight and we had all of it just like that. I think that clearly illustrates that managers aren't always clear on what we can do.

JIT KEE CHIN

Chief Data and Innovation Officer

Interviewer: How should different levels of the company (data scientists, business owners and leadership) help with data or digital transformation?

Jit Kee: Leadership needs to set an aspiration and direction, then assess – ideally in quantifiable terms – what benefit they'd like to achieve. Then, a credible cross-functional digital transformation leader should work in close partnership with business leaders to create a roadmap. It's critical to choose a few quick wins where those business leaders are strong champions, delivering value at the outset. It's also important to focus efforts; depending on the size of the business, it may make sense to start with the transformation of one business unit and then use that success to grow momentum.

Data scientists and other technical roles need to learn to work across functions, ideally in project teams where success of the individual is directly linked to success of the different digital projects. Other employees need to be curious about digital and technology advancements that help with efficiencies or better decision making and put effort into learning new ways of working.

Interviewer: Which business models and value chain changes does data-driven transformation make possible?

Jit Kee: There are several examples of business model changes. Digitization of workflows, especially workflows like procurement, can give rise to platform-based business models that are similar to what Amazon has. The standardization of data structures through digitization creates a valuable data asset that can be monetized in the future – think of data-as-an-asset, benchmarks and analytical insights. Data services represent another business model change, which includes helping others navigate similar data challenges. Finally, data-based business models along the technical stack, such as industry-specific data integrators, also become possible.

In each of these instances, the value chain also shifts. These changes may make space for a new digital player, cut out middlemen or other intermediaries, or enable existing players to offer new products and services and enter adjacent sectors.

Interviewer: Which gaps have you seen in the data transformation journey and how far has the organization come in addressing them?

Jit Kee: Change management and adoption remain the most time-consuming steps in the transformation journey. We've come quite a long way, but they're never done.

Interviewer: What has been the most important aspect of building data-centric teams compared to other types of teams?

Jit Kee: There are two key building blocks for data-centric teams: insight and usage. Insight refers to what the data are telling us. Usage is who is looking at the data and managing the outcome, and how they're approaching those results.

What's been challenging is finding data professionals that have three essential characteristics: the ability to use the advanced tools, strong business acumen and knowledge of what truly matters and a deep curiosity to understand what the numbers are telling us. Once the path is set, the next major challenge is finding change professionals who are good at influencing others and driving an effective adoption program.

Interviewer: What advice do you have for C-Level leaders seeking to overcome resistance to data transformation?

Jit Kee: Break down the full transformation into realistic phases, with consistent delivery of quick wins. It is unlikely you will transform the enterprise overnight, so it is important to celebrate success along the way.

Be clear with your commitment to the transformation and over-communicate successes, phrasing them in terms of their impact on the business.

Demonstrate your commitment with big moves in resource allocation, both in terms of finances and talent. It's often harder to remove key talent from their day jobs than it is to reallocate capital, but both approaches are important.

Understand that you will not convert everyone at once, and that's OK. There is a natural adoption curve for technology.

Interviewer: Any pitfalls and best practices you would like to share?

Jit Kee: There is no substitute for top digital talent. The talent landscape for digital roles is now mature, so you have a deep pool to choose from. Also, always be very deliberate about the buy/build/partner choice. You do not need to build everything internally, and the right partnerships make all the difference.

RAHUL BHARGAVA

*Assistant Professor – Data Literacy, Journalism,
Design & Civic Tech*

Interviewer: How would you describe what you do on a day-to-day basis? Can you also talk about digital transformation in a broader context?

Rahul: Right now, my work focuses on finding different ways to integrate the changes that are happening around data, particularly computationally mediated and captured data, the impact it has on society and rethink some of those processes to focus on power and participation.

Interviewer: Could you speak a bit more about what power and participation encompasses?

Rahul: So, when I think about power, I think about the ability to authentically engage and change the circumstances for oneself or for a community that they're involved in. That typically for me is trying to *democratize rather than centralize power*.

Interviewer: This is interesting because some regimes have taken the opposite stance in terms of democratization.

Rahul: I mean if we look at most businesses that have succeeded in various forms of what one calls digital adoption or transformation, they often have a *combination of top-down and bottom-up approaches*. If you look at data and the changes that are happening over the last 15 years, I would say that 80–90% of data initiatives in larger or midsized companies are housed in IT departments. You want something that everyone in your company is going to adopt to come out of it. If you want people to adopt a data-centric way of thinking then you're going to have the IT person come and run a training. People don't take a step back and think and that's what I mean about power. It is a top-down play whereas when you see things like rich media document editing 30 years ago or smart-phones, they are two examples that came more from the bottom-up approach where people brought those tools into the workplace and the workplace adapted to support and augment and take partial ownership of those tools to the point where you'll see mobile tool adoption from the top down and you'll see it pushed from the bottom up.

Interviewer: I think of this like the YouTube revolution where a lot of the people are posting such high-quality content and ironically, when you talk about Macbooks and the new hardware devices being released, the people who are pushing them the most are the people editing 4K YouTube videos and pushing the M1 Mac Pro GPU to the limit. There are thousands of these people every day posting videos with semi-professional if not professional level content that can compete with the quality of some of these full-blown advertising agencies.

Rahul: So, YouTube has two faces. One is like a broadcast platform and the other a messaging platform. The one you're talking about is the one where they make most of their money. This is how they get their monopoly. This is where they get most of their power.

Interviewer: So that's the power part of it. Can you speak more about the participation?

Rahul: My lens for thinking about this is data transformation and digital data transformation. I just finished a book chapter about this, about how the processes are historical, extractive and capitalist based. When a business wants to work with data, it's usually thinking about how to use data to measure this person's performance and evaluate it. Like how can I help this person use data to do their job better so when you roll out a data initiative, people are not like "Oh no, I don't want to collect that data, you're going to use it to fire me." Why would anybody participate in this? So you drive participation by rethinking power. If you can align your goals such that the person wants to use data to be able to do their job better, and you can then use that data to look across your whole business to see how it's going and if those are in alignment, then everybody wins. That is one of the things where it's really about how businesses in many cases think about what data are for, and I think that some of the patterns embedded in data are historically extractive. Also, what these data are about is made intentionally opaque. So, it's like being a lawyer. Like I can't participate in my legal defense because I can't speak that language and I can't participate in this data analysis because I don't speak that language, and that's a problem. My research works on this very directly.

Interviewer: To your point, IT departments are famous for making things opaque because that's their power. Could you give classic examples of failures and contrasting success to really drive this point home. Maybe an example of a change case that didn't work because of obvious power centralization in a stereotypical context of IT departments as you mentioned earlier.

Rahul: This is pushing me further out of my comfort zone because I don't work in corporate contexts as much, but the one that I would highlight again from my wheelhouse of data as a digital transformation tool is the KPI dashboard. Dashboarding is a summary of data about something that's created so that higher ups can somehow get an insight without understanding the full context of something about a lot of things happening under them. That's kind of the point of a dashboard with KPI indicators and that's very disempowering to the person whose one data point gets summed up in a pie chart with 10,000 other ones. I get the argument that we could give a picture of everything that's happening but it ignores the human elements of that social process. Even if you end up with a similar result, the messaging around it is that it serves the decision makers that are in a small room instead of distributing ideas and decision making across a whole set of people.

Interviewer: So what could be some approaches, whether it's in a corporate environment or in a social environment that could make it better?

Rahul: I like things where you have a giant screen in the same room where a lot of people are working on the same thing being represented on the screen. So, there's a shared ownership of what feels like a mirror for us and not a window of somebody looking down at us from outside. That mirror is an example of a version that creates a very different narrative. If we're seeing all of our work up there then there's a sense of shared ownership that could be cultivated. So sometimes there are social changes that are very small that work within business language and structure and then having something that talks about that not in a punitive way, but like, "oh OK, here's a trend we're seeing, help me understand this trend" but not "here's a trend we're seeing you need to work harder on." So much of it is just social. When we talk a lot about digital transformation of this and that, the language is broken. If we deploy technology somewhere then that's not what you're doing. What you're doing is integrating it because there's some social process already and your technology will be integrated into that social process. You're not just parachuting it somewhere, it's totally the wrong way of thinking about it. So, even our language to talk about this is broken. So it really starts with having a bad way of communicating about it.

Interviewer: Digital transformation sounds very hierarchical. It sounds very top down to me when I hear that term. So are there other terms that we can use other than, say, even digital transformation?

Rahul: In digital transformation, the agency is on digital, not on the thing being transformed. So I think you're spot on there in thinking this isn't capturing what we mean. Integration is a term that I just used, so when you integrate something there's two parties. What is the other one in your case? Is it a business culture or a business practice that is being transformed? I would encourage you to think about that question because you could have a lot of answers that are all valid, but which one you care about most can guide you into a terminology that better reflects your ideas and *what's the thing being Transformed.*

Interviewer: Thanks for that. That's quite insightful. If you could have one message to pass to some of these companies that are famously trying to transform digitally, and you've covered a lot of ground already regarding how it shouldn't be too centralized and that it should be more inclusive. So, is there a common message we could communicate to say this is probably the way to do it that's going to be faster, cheaper, better and more effective in the long term?

Rahul: I think it's one that's obvious but isn't practiced that well. If you believe in the model of technology being integrated into some social process or some business process, then you don't know what's going to happen until that integration starts. So, you might build something and then people will start using it and then it turns into something else. So, *the earlier you can start iterating on that cycle, the better off you are.* That way it's the narrative where you identify your most risky assumption, and you build something that focuses on that. Try it out with the people that are going to use it. It's good human computer interaction design and this is the narrative that so many design schools build and push out. For any process that involves some kind of digital technology being integrated into some workflow or a business plan or process, I think trying out and planning for an iterative cycle of integration is the right way to do it, and the earlier you can start that, the better it'll be, because also it creates shared ownership.

Interviewer: If I'm interpreting correctly, this is consistent with what some of the formalized design thinking programs have been doing.

Rahul: Exactly. It's user-centered design and arguing that's not just a way to design a technology, it's a way to design the process of using the technology.

Interviewer: So, you're not trying to get a solution stamped on the company, you're trying to build a solution within the company from the ground up, right?

Rahul: Yes, because when you're integrating you're using something with someone and then that's someone that you're using it with. It creates shared ownership where they have part of that ownership of the thing once it's ready to roll out to a larger set because they're like "Oh yeah, I tried that out once, it sucked. Maybe it's better now."

We should say that at least they feel like they were a part of it. This is what design school students learn in user-centered design 101, and it's rarely practiced because it doesn't fit some economic models.

Interviewer: I think as you know, sadly a lot of the practices in large companies is once the train leaves the station it's just going down that line.

Rahul: Yeah, but we talk about nimbleness all the time in businesses and they want to be nimble. So they just need to practice that nimbleness in lots of different settings, including the technology integration one. You can tell where I'm coming from, that's my narrative.

CANSU CANCA

Founder & Director, AI Ethics Lab
Ethics Lead & Research Associate Professor, Institute for
Experiential AI

Interviewer: Before we get into your transformation, could you tell us a little bit about yourself?

Cansu: I'm a philosopher by training and my concentration has been on applied ethics from the start. I worked for a long time on bioethics and moved on to AI and digital via health technologies. In bioethics, we analyze ethical questions in relation to the physician, the patient and the healthcare system. But there are increasingly more AI tools integrated into healthcare with ethically loaded decisions built into them. I was troubled by the fact that as ethicists, we were not discussing any of those ethical decisions that these tools bring into healthcare. In fact, we didn't have any idea on what's going on inside these tools and how they were structured. So that was my motivation. I wasn't actually planning to move on to the digital space. But as I looked more and more into it, I realized that there are a lot of ethical questions that are very interesting in terms of digitalization in all areas, not just health, and the development and use of AI technologies. While I work on various specific ethical questions related to AI, I particularly focus on how we can implement and integrate ethics into innovation.

Interviewer: What gave you the motivation to walk this path?

Cansu: One of the motivations was well, can we do this better – better than the current ways that we practice ethics? Can we do this right this time? The most well-established practice of ethics is in research ethics with its principles laid out in the Belmont Report, codified in Common Rule, and a whole system of IRB boards structured around it. I don't think this particular model of ethics practice (we can call it the "ethics oversight model") is a good one. But if not the ethics oversight model, then what? How should we integrate ethics into innovation? I think before, we were living in a state of blissful ignorance. Like, physicians were happy that they now have a technology that can predict a disease before it starts and patients were happy to have robotics assist in their surgery. But once we start realizing the problems like, well, the predictive algorithm can be discriminatory, or the robotic assistants can create a responsibility gap, then the questions started. Are we doing this right? Are there more questions that should be asked from the physician's, from the patient's, from the health system's perspectives as they engage with these tools?

Interviewer: So if I could ask what kind of say, expected or unexpected responses to introduction of these digital transformation measures that you observe or notice in those environments?

Cansu: I'm not sure if it is expected or unexpected, but I think the main thing that was striking was that they were very quickly adopted without many questions. The main assumption appeared to be: the algorithm is mathematical, so it must be right; or if it is robotic, it must be precise. Which is of course not always the case.

Interviewer: In that context, what role were you serving at that time when you noticed these things? Were you a consultant or part of the hospital system?

Cansu: I was a medical ethics lecturer at a medical school. Basically, I was designing and running the whole medical ethics curriculum for the Faculty of Medicine at the University of Hong Kong.

Interviewer: What have you seen organizations doing that worked well and didn't work so well?

Cansu: Honestly, that's not a very happy question in the sense that usually nothing really goes so well. I started this in 2016 while I was still in Hong Kong and the problem was that back then for a very long time nobody really understood when I said there are ethical issues in AI that we need to deal with. The reception was often "Let's just not mess with the technology – it's mathematical, it should be OK," and "if we 'add' ethics, it's just going to mess up the system, so we shouldn't even engage in the ethical aspect of the technology." It took a while and multiple examples to explain that ethics is not an "addition" but rather a built-in aspect of all technology. Only recently, "technology is not value-neutral" became a common knowledge, or at least more widely known.

Interviewer: Why did organizations think that way?

Cansu: First, I think it was some sort of ignorance,

"We don't need this because the system is mathematical, and we are not doing anything bad with it. We are not using it maliciously, so there cannot be anything unethical about it." Once it was pointed out by researchers and the media that ethical decisions are already embedded into the system often resulting in preventable harm and injustices, they started to go like "There is a real rush to move towards digitalization and we don't want to be left behind. We'll take care of ethics later once we have the technology. We have to first have the technology developed and start using it and see if it works. And then we can look at the ethical aspects of it." By then, of course it's too late, because multiple ethics decisions are already embedded into the technology. I mean it can be done, you can still unearth, analyze, and fix the ethical issues in the technology and in its use, but it's just much more resource intensive to do this later on.

Interviewer: So what has changed?

Cansu: I think now, finally, organizations/companies are realizing that ethical issues are inescapable and they have to deal with them, preferably from the beginning and preferably before they are picked up by the researchers and by the media. But I can still not say that they are doing it right. I think the good part is that now there's more awareness. They are putting in place dedicated teams, so that is a big plus. Previously, the ethical concerns were raised only at grassroots level, and that didn't go anywhere because the leadership was not interested. Now, there is an interest both from the leadership and from grassroots. And they are trying to work it out.

Interviewer: So initially it was the grassroots were the ones pushing for ethical consideration, and then later on the leadership sort of caught up, if you like?

Cansu: Yes, exactly.

Interviewer: I want to dig a bit deeper there. Why did leadership become interested?

Cansu: I actually don't know the leadership's motivation. My guess would be that well, now AI ethics is a topic in the spotlight, and if you don't want to embarrass yourself and lose public trust, you need to catch up. And if you lose trust, you might lose the data – no one cannot afford losing data, so they better don't lose trust. That's my cynical and probably realistic guess. I mean, it could also be a genuine interest and concern about the ethical impact of the technologies that they are developing and deploying – but we will never know. Even when we talk to leaders, I guess we cannot necessarily know their genuine motivations.

Interviewer: And you said you've seen plans, which things are there in the plans? And which things are typically lacking from your perspective?

Cansu: So one thing that's usually there is AI ethics principles. AI principles are in every organization's AI ethics section and I never understand how they became such a trend – especially since they often seem to be vague and not operational. AI ethics principles also follow this research ethics model. The principlism framework created in research ethics put forth three core principles that basically reflect the whole of moral and political theories in philosophy: respect autonomy, minimize harm and maximize benefits and do justice. And then you have instrumental principles such as privacy, transparency, accountability that enable these three core principles. The problem with principles (with any principle-based framework) is that they are usually too general and vague, and in complex cases, they necessarily conflict. So there is only so much guidance you can receive from principles. That is not to say that they are not useful – a carefully constructed set of AI ethics principles can help organizations make better and more consistent decisions.

Interviewer: What differentiates one company from the other in terms of AI ethics principles?

Cansu: The point of having a specific set of AI principles for an organization is not to be as comprehensive as possible but rather to provide guidance on which principles to prioritize if and when it is not possible to satisfy them all. For example, it is better if an AI system protects privacy and ensures transparency. Yet, in some cases, these two principles will conflict – it may not be possible to satisfy them both. The organizational AI ethics principles can guide us in which one to prioritize by emphasizing one and not the other. Again, this is only when the conflict is inevitable, otherwise we always want to satisfy them all. A good example for carefully constructing organizational AI principles comes from the Department of Defense (DoD). The DoD explained their choice of principles saying what they don't include is what they don't want to endorse. So they intentionally and explicitly decided what not to include; and they decided not to include fairness, arguing that "fights should not be fair, as DoD aims to create the conditions to maintain an unfair advantage over any potential adversaries." This intentional decision making on value trade-offs is necessary for making sense of organization-specific AI ethics principles and it is not common among organizations. They often simply pick and choose whatever principle feels and sounds good. They would put privacy in their document but not transparency, and when you ask them why, they wouldn't really know. Their answer should be "because when it comes to a conflict between privacy and transparency, we as a company make a claim that we are valuing privacy over transparency. That's why we did not put transparency." Only if created with such thought, company-specific principles make sense.

Interviewer: I wonder whether companies can do it at the project level. So, for instance, if there is a conflict between two principles, this is what we're going to prioritize for this project.

Cansu: They should do it. They should know all the relevant principles and try to fulfill them all because that would be the ethically best outcome. Only when they face an inescapable conflict, then they should turn to the company-specific principles and say, well, you know we already decided that we are going to prioritize this value over this other one when there's a conflict. And that's what we are basing our decision in this project.

Interviewer: What kind of people should be appointed for a specific position in the company?

Cansu: First of all, an ethics expert has to be a moral philosopher. In practice, this seems to be absurdly controversial. It's simple – your legal expert needs to be a lawyer, your AI expert needs to be an AI scientist and your ethics expert needs to be a moral philosopher (which means an ethicist). Ethics is a discipline with its own methods and body of knowledge; it's not just an object of inquiry or interest. So if you have an ethics team made only from computer scientists, anthropologists and lawyers, you simply do not have an ethics expert in that team. The second question is about the structure of your ethics staff. While several companies now have a Chief Ethics Officer and an Ethics team, they miss a whole network of people. You cannot have a single person or even just a team that flags, detects and solves all ethical questions. In addition to your ethics experts, you also need designated ethics respondents within teams that can flag issues, engage with the available guidance, and even solve some of the non-complex ethics issues. And if the issue is complex, they can escalate it to the ethics team or an ethics advisory board. A board meets only at certain times. So you have to have these intermediaries, who are connected to each other in different roles and skilled for their respective roles within the company to handle the simple questions without waiting for a board's input and escalate only the complex ones.

Interviewer: That is fascinating. So you need people that are seen as very confident within their department whether it's engineering or some other field that then say, you know this project we're now doing raises ethical issues. And then they can get the information and escalate it if it's needed.

Cansu: When I talk to the innovation teams and ask them "when you have an ethics problem, what do you do?" they usually say, "we are discussing it within the team." Then I ask: "Is anybody qualified to discuss it within the team?" They answer "No, but we brainstorm." So, there is a critical question related to the technology which may impact individual's lives and the builders of this technology do not connect with someone qualified to figure out this question, ensure that they reduce harm, manipulation or discrimination. And whatever happens in this brainstorming session, there is no proper documentation of the discussion or its outcome. So there is no way to look back and check these decisions later either. If you have someone who has the skill, at least to mediate this, then we could at least have a documentation of the process, the reasoning and the outcome to check and perhaps fix retrospectively.

Interviewer: Are there particular companies or industries that are known to do this?

Cansu: In my experience, there is not huge differences among companies. I have not worked with them directly but it seems like Microsoft is one of those companies that strive to do AI ethics properly. Not only they are one of the early movers but they also have been building their ethics infrastructure steadily. They seem to be actually putting in place proper processes and structures, including an AI Ethics Board. I'm always worried about copying the research ethics model with principles and boards but if used well, I think a board can serve a valuable function. I would have expected finance and health to be the leading industries in AI ethics because they have all these previous experiences with comprehensive ethical and regulatory systems and use cases, but this was not the case.

Interviewer: So which do you think is the worst category or the worst industries that you would most like to kind of shake them up and say hey! Private universities?

Cansu: I'm not sure if it is sector bound. If I have to give an answer, I would say military and criminal justice (including the law enforcement), because the stakes are so high. The good thing is that both industries are indeed doing quite a lot of work on AI ethics. They are still not there, but at least they seem to be now aware of the importance of AI ethics and interested in getting it right. Of course, this awareness did not just happen – law enforcement, for example, received a lot of backlash for facial recognition tools and only then they started to engage with the ethical impact of these tools. I guess better late than never.

Interviewer: You mentioned that a board is sometimes not the best way to go and I remember when the media covered the AI ethics panel that Google put together that lasted less than a couple of hours. Is it the case that some companies are doing this to get public recognition because this is not the intermediary network we're talking about?

Cansu: I think it lasted a week. I do think that there is a strategic function of a board if it's structured and utilized well. So you can have a leadership level board that decides on the company strategy in AI ethics. You know when we talk about these value trade-offs, for example, what does your company endorse? What would be their principles? It would be good to have a board to deal with these over-arching questions. Or if you are dealing with a really high-risk project, it would be good to run this by a high level board. As you see, I'm talking about a strategic board in some sense, not a review board. A review board becomes a bottleneck, which slows down the operations to a pain-ful degree. And they are neither engaged enough to look at the projects properly, nor high level enough to set the strategy. So they are these weird creatures of gatekeeping – yet often they also don't have the right expertise to fulfill that function. So I do think that boards can play a useful role, but in practice they are often not set up to do so. And in terms of companies getting public recognition for their ethics "moves," I think a lot of the first reactions such as putting together these AI ethics boards or publishing the AI ethics principles have been just "ethics washing" – so, only for show.

Interviewer: So you've also given us a lot of advice implic-itly about what could be done with intermediaries who are more engaged with the daily tasks. What steps are being taken or should be to be taken to accelerate this adoption of not just ethical practices, but in general the approach in organizations, beyond incorporating education, incorpo-rating training, officially designating roles. What seems to be the way forward here?

Cansu: I think all of them. We need to decide where to start, what to prioritize. We do this by assessing the company's current level of engagement with ethics and creating a roadmap for them. For example, if a company that is building IoTs say that their job does not involve ethics, then for that company, we probably should start with raising awareness. On the other hand, if a company is launching, for example, a new surveillance tool, then we should immediately jump to an ethics analysis, trying to detect and eliminate as much ethics risks as possible before the tool goes to the market. So we have to know the company's starting point to define the best course of action. But taken as a whole, there has to be a lot of raising awareness. Because most people concerned about ethics are thinking about it more in terms of "be a nice person and have a good moral compass." It's more like a Sunday school mindset rather than an analytic assessment and procedure. Showing that ethics is systematic and analytic is also very useful for connecting with engineers, and this is something that we have been doing a lot in our workshops. Next would be to start creating a comprehensive AI ethics strategy for companies, which would include building their guiding materials and tools, designating ethics roles and incorporating trainings and putting in place processes to integrate ethics analyses into their innovation cycle.

Interviewer: So communicate the ethical practices or issues in the language or style of the audience? Like engineers appreciate a systematic approach because that's closer to their psyche. But then you mentioned way back that in the healthcare field, people said "oh, this is mathematical, so it must be right." So it wasn't in their language, which led them to actually adopt algorithms more quickly, perhaps incorrectly.

Cansu: Physicians, as most people, see the computer as this objective, mathematical truth teller. Judges and police are other examples of that – if the system can provide them with a risk assessment, for example, they seem to believe that they don't need more information. I mean an engineer can tell you that's not really correct, because there are many other ways they can and could have built the risk assessment tool. As developers of the technology, they know that many uncertain decisions go into creating these tools. What developers and users don't necessarily know is: which decisions were ethically relevant? For example, what proxies did they use which correspond to existing ethical issues in the domain? One famous example is this Science article[2] where they show that a commercially used risk assessment tool used health cost as a proxy for the health need. And the problem is that, well, the society spends very little on Black patients in comparison to white patients. If you don't know this existing ethical issue in healthcare, you might not realize this proxy is imperfect and worse, discriminatory. Fixing this bias resulted in increasing "the percentage of Black patients receiving additional help from 17.7 to 46.5%." Everybody knows the correlation between ZIP code and race, but other ethical connections and underlying ethical issues are harder to detect for those who are not familiar with the domain. So knowing the ethical landscape of the domain informs you on what to look for to ensure that the technology does not perpetuate existing ethical problems or create new ones. And engineers don't necessarily realize which components correspond to the ethically relevant input.

Interviewer: So it is key to understand how the audience thinks about it, and that's challenging.

Cansu: Once the developers know that these are the ways that the ethical value decisions come into play and sneak into the technology, then it's much easier for them to grasp ethics. Then we start talking each other's language and we can collaborate on solving these ethical issues. Once they understand what is ethically loaded, they can be vigilant – if they are not sure whether what they are doing is ethically reliable; then they can raise a flag and say, "let's check this, let's take a minute." And they should be the ones who need to raise this flag because you don't want to put an ethicist in every single team of the organization

Interviewer: Nothing would get done! Just kidding …

Cansu: Also, they would hate ethicists! That would be like the IRBs all over again – researchers are not thrilled to deal with IRBs and honestly, I can relate to that. In research ethics, we have a plenty bad reputation. We don't want to create more anger unnecessarily! But seriously, ethics should be a dynamic and integrated part of innovation – not a distinct policing exercise that is imposed on innovators.

Interviewer: You talked about positioning the message in a way that mirrors, or at least fits, the people who are supposed to adopt it. I wonder what would have been the approach for physicians? Because getting them to adopt it quickly is one thing, but getting to adopt it properly is another thing.

Cansu: Here, we move from the developers to the "professional" users – like the physician, the police officer, the judge, and so on. These are the users of technology in their respective professions. The responsibility falls both on the developers and on the "professional" users in making sure that the technology is used ethically. In talking about ethics and building technologies ethically; the dashboard gets the least attention. What information are you providing to the police officer, for example, with that tool? What is on the user interface? How do you expect the officer to make a rational decision engaging with the tool? Because if the user interface does not convey the necessary information in an appropriate format, we cannot expect professionals, who are not engineers, to have a rational engagement with these systems. They cannot rationally disagree with the system. We are basically providing them with tools that say "here's the outcome, take it or leave it – no more questions." Such a tool is not designed responsibly and cannot be used responsibly. As a police officer or as a physician, you might think that the system is making the wrong risk calculation, but you cannot really say how or why – you can only say "I have a different hunch." Instead, what we need to provide them with is a much better structure for human computer interaction, where the professionals, who are experts in their field should be able to go back to the dashboard, go back to the user interface of the application and say "I don't think this person is high risk. What were the variables that you took into account for getting to that outcome?" Only when we understand the system, we can talk about reasonable engagement with the system.

JON HAY

*Vice President, Data, Intelligence
and Analytics*

Interviewer: Can you tell us a little bit about what you do or have done either with the Red Sox or thereabouts with data transformation and other things.

Jon: My title is data intelligence and analytics. I oversee everything from the moment we're ingesting data from various third party sources to the moment that we are deploying it to our end users including sales, marketing, ticketing, operations folks. Half my team is on the IT side. We have a data architect, a data reporting developer, a Salesforce analyst who works on ingesting data, ETL and a variety of cloud and database aspects. I have an analytics team in charge of taking all the information from ingestion that then cleanse, deduplicates, etc., and from there converts it into actionable insights. These insights include what should be charged for tickets, who should be called to try and sell tickets, what we charge for a beer or when should we have certain games. What time of day? What day of week? Dynamic pricing is an important area along with other ventures including a 5,000 seat Music Hall right behind the bleachers in Fenway Park. A lot of the P&L around that was on our team. You can think of it as soup to nuts and we're an internal consulting arm which means rather than having analysts on our sales team and our marketing team we're the centralized resource that supports all those teams that tries to ultimately, take a bunch of all of this information and put it into whatever format, whether that be a PowerPoint, a Tableau report, some analysis, a bunch of customer records scored with a number and whatever is most useful for them to do their job.

Interviewer: So you have a bunch of internal clients that are always wanting your services. How do you prioritize requests? Do you have a system for this?

Jon: It is a huge challenge for us, but one thing I'm very big on – The two by two matrix and I'm living up here in the high impact, low effort area. Requests that can really move the needle in the short term we try to never let go into the bottom left quadrant. I think sometimes, especially in the IT world, people get distracted by shiny objects and find that there's a really interesting challenge that will take a long time, but maybe not that impactful. It's working with stakeholders and saying – we do see your point and with 150 internal customers and everyone's project can't always be the highest priority, right? Because to them it is absolutely important, and part of my job as the president in the department was to have those frank conversations. Here's other things that are coming out of people in your department, right? Or people adjacent to you? How do we think about what the priority order is? And by the way, how can we maybe align some of these things. Premium sales needs an inventory management tool to manage our sweet inventory, but Fenway events is an inventory management tool to manage all of the different days and assess they could be put on the same timeline, build one massive inventory management tool in salesforce and deliver that to both customers at the same time. So definitely trying to work smarter, not harder, and we certainly heavily leverage any resources because we're a pretty small team and we do make heavy use of the Northeastern Co-op program. We have a rotating Co-op on our data reporting team. We just started up a new Co-op on our CRM team so we try and find as many resources as we can to throw out problems.

It is a real challenge and sometimes you have to give a difficult answer. Which is, the answer is "no." Just realistically, it's not. You know it's not. It's true, it's in this bottom left quadrant and so you know our chambers can't handle it and that's been a challenge for me, our senior executive may say, we're in the business of yes, the answer is always yes and we all agree with that until you realize you can't say yes to everyone. Also, you can't say no to everyone, so that's definitely a challenge for us to think through that.

Interviewer: This is a classic use case for the Research Lab at Northeastern that's always looking for pie in the sky projects from organizations. A classic case a company analytics group that has only got 10 people on staff that would like to try a new classification algorithm, but it's a funky new deep learning project that can't be done right now, so let's give it to this research lab at Northeastern. We can talk about that a bit later. How long have you been in this area?

Jon: Almost nine.

Interviewer: Nine years?

Jon: I'm nine seasons. We're a season based team here. Actually, I was an intern here for two years.

Interviewer: How have things changed? What are the big changes in terms of getting things done in terms of data-centric decision making since you joined.

Jon: I'll speak to the business side and I can certainly speak to some to the Baseball side as well. I spent a couple of years 2013 and 2014, I was a baseball analytics build-ing predictive models for player performance, context analysis, things like that. I got pitched on transitioning to the business side in 2015 because we literally didn't have anyone doing that. We weren't dynamically pricing our tickets. We weren't thinking about basically all the stuff that we do that every regular non-baseball company does. We just weren't doing it right. You know, these teams are run by very successful people who don't need revenue from their teams to pay their mortgage. They are billion-aires who may not feel the need to run a sports team at maximum efficiency In 2015, we had no data warehouse. We didn't even have the people to build that. We had to hire a data architect we didn't have anyone on our IT department right. If the email or phone system goes down, that was our IT department. Everything I'm telling you now about all of this process all happened for us in the last five years and even now, with us moving to the cloud that's escalated significantly. We're working much closer with Google and we're thinking about AI opportunities. It really is night and day and some of that is a little more of a statement about how behind sports teams are compared to other industries. There really has been a huge adoption on the business side the last five or six years for us.

Interviewer: At that 2015 point, would you say the Red Sox were indicative of the baseball franchise industry, or were they behind other franchises on this?

Jon: Definitely indicative. I would say they were in American major sports. You think about the 120-ish teams in the four major sports. There were probably two or three teams that were really putting this thinking toward things that were using data analytics on the business side. It really wasn't a thing. To the extent that these things were being done, they were being done by hand. Pricing was getting a bunch of people in a room and looking at a bunch of games and discussing which to not knock off, if it's effective or efficient. But you know sports is a copycat industry. Once clubs started hiring people with analytics backgrounds with MBAs and computer scientists, and people from management consulting coming over, suddenly owners are all looking around and saying: "Where do I get my Harvard MBA that comes in and rethinks my entire business model." It really has been just in the last four or five years. They're certainly not as far along as we are. But almost everyone now has at least some department who is tasked with using a data-driven approach to solve business side problems.

Interviewer: At this point, where would you put the Red Sox in the hierarchy of being ahead of the curve?

Jon: I would say it within baseball we're probably in the 80–90th percentile in terms of where we are or within the industry at large. If you include biotech and consumer packaged goods I think we're probably 30th percentile. Some of the stuff that we think is cutting edge here. It's always funny for us. We rolled out dynamic pricing this year, and now every seat can have a different price. We change it over time, feeding in a bunch of data, running predictions. Yet, the airline industry has been doing this for 35 years. Well, JetBlue does it at orders of magnitude greater scale than we do so. Granted, they don't have to deal with the same weather, starting pitchers and other game stuff, but we do often point out that I think this is one of the nice things for us. I worked in finance before this. Our CTO was at the weather channel. For 20 years, when people come in from other industries and we say, oh, actually, this is how other things are being done elsewhere. It's not rocket science, but it seems like rocket science to people that have spent their whole career in sports. We haven't had that outside perspective, so it's been an opportunity for me and others to come in. We can cherry pick a lot of the things that other industries are doing well and try and apply those things to our own business.

Interviewer: So from the inspiration and the talent you got back when you started this in 2015 versus now, can you characterize it back then? Where did you find people and expertise? How are you finding talent now considering the competitive nature and poaching them might be going on?

Jon: Yeah you know it's funny when I hired my first analyst, I basically reached out to all the local schools and said hey, I'm looking for this job but I didn't post it on the Internet. We reached out to schools and found someone through that. These days we're going nationwide, we're going international. We're posting jobs everywhere, LinkedIn, teamwork, online. I would say early on was hard. It was easier to find that Jack of all trades, because we had so many holes to fill. I could bring in someone that wasn't necessarily a data scientist, but are a hard core statistician. But to do a lot of things well, they could learn new things and could communicate well, a little bit more of a "five tool player." Now I feel when I'm hiring, I'm filling a very specific need because we want to build out the department. I'm looking for someone that can do a very specific thing very well and to your point, that's where it starts to get tricky. Especially now as sports has not re-invented work in the last couple of years and with a lot of jobs going remote it's gotten harder for us. We just recently hired an analyst on our team and for the first time we had a hard time at the end to convince people.

Sports doesn't always pay well. What we sell is the opportunity to get to go to baseball games and hopefully win some World Series tickets and so when you're competing for technical talent that knows what they're worth, and they can go to literally anywhere, regardless of location. If you want to work in sports, there is a 50% pay cut. That's what we're coming up against. It's actually been an effort for us to convince our senior executives – "Hey look, if you want these sorts of people, to hire data architects you gotta pay market rate." I mean, you're not going to find those people to work in sports just because it's the Red Sox right? I think to go back to your question, five years ago you could do that. You could get those people because of the dream job factor. More recently that's been a challenge for us, and something had to adjust to just in terms of compensation in the way that we approach those rules.

Interviewer: In talking about leadership, what are the different opportunities that you have with the different stakeholders in the business? In other words, what does leadership really have to do to help digital information transformation in a company?

Jon: My boss is a good example of this. He's a CFO and a very smart guy with dozens of direct reports and a lot of responsibilities. His goal is to be conversational about a lot of things right. He tells me: "Look, I'm not going to understand absolutely every aspect of data architecture or the cloud, but if the boss our team president, asks me if we should we invest another half a million dollars in our cloud architecture, I need a one minute pitch to tell him that the answer is 'yes'." I don't need to know why because I trust you, Jon and your team, but I think a lot of it comes down to making sure that you can give people those tools that have the ability to look at the end result. You have to get a lot of trust because you're not going to ask senior executives to understand some of these things around data transformation and you know the ways that we deliver things, but you do want them to buy into what you're doing because it's not cheap. Whether it's personnel or third parties or tools. It's not cheap and to be able to speak eloquently enough that if push comes to shove and we have to defend something at a budget, you don't have to call me into a room to come running in breathlessly with a giant flow chart that explains how our data structure is a big part of it and we're very fortunate that my boss is an MIT alum. He was a consultant, he's got that background and so he does have a very analytical mind. Even though he doesn't do all that stuff directly he always picks these things up and is very understanding of the stuff that we're doing and is very supportive.

Interviewer: The people you hire have to do with data science and apart from these skills, what other skills or traits are beneficial?

Jon: I do think so much of it is the ability to communicate with people who may be skeptical of what you're doing. When I hire new people, the first thing I would say is don't walk into a meeting with a bunch of your code, don't walk into a meeting and run a Python script. You need to think about who you're presenting. I think my phrase is always the technical skills are necessary but not sufficient? Sometimes we get these young people, they've gone through a great curriculum in a place such as Northeastern University. They come in and have all the bells and whistles and they can do this and that. Then you have to work with them and say okay, but here's how you put a finished product out. The goal is not to have the best model, it's not a problem set. The goal is to affect change and sometimes the way you affect change has nothing to do with the quality of the model but everything with the quality of the pitch and the way that you communicate. A lot of my job is funny in retrospect. Actually most of my job is hiring really smart people to do the work and then my job is to understand I'm at the center of all this. How do we communicate that effectively such that we can actually not walk in a room and someone throws up their hands and says I don't know what the heck this is?

Interviewer: A closing question. If you think about the current state at the Red Sox, would you say the approach is fully integrated into the business yet? Is it 80% there? Is it something that really, as you said, they trust what your team is doing? They don't fully get it but they get the why ...

Jon: It's a great question. I would say where we are good is internal capital. We are at the point where almost every team we work with has a lot of trust. We are at about 75%. Now the last 25% is really around some automation. So much of what we do is manual we're building predictions and taking output and manually entering it into a variety of systems. A lot of our effort to the cloud was really about dynamic pricing instead of having a model that makes us constantly push recommendations. All this customer journey stuff is a good example. Why are we putting together lists of people receive emails? All that should be rules based and data driven. My team is 8 people. I could keep 28 people busy. It's how do we take all the great work that's being done deliver more of it without hiring 20 more people. That's really about ML. It's about AI, it's about how do you turn that stuff into these things that are just running at all times and delivering the insights to people. You know, you're steering the runner instead of you know, paddling right the boat.

Interviewer: Well this is great. Talking to you is like talking to a guy running a startup that's really exciting again.

Jon: It's so funny, I always say I feel I'm working here in a series A or series B funded startup because everyone is wearing a lot of hats. Everything works, but a lot is manual. If we have a doubleheader in between the two games the whole front office goes and cleans the stadium. It's that startup mentality, right?

Interviewer: It certainly is.

Jon: Yeah, so as somebody said that because it's totally right and that's what I love about it. One of the things I love is I did some startup stuff in a business school and I love that passion and that excitement. It really is at an early stage startup sometimes.

DANIELA DE AGUIAR

Senior Analyst

Interviewer: Thanks, Daniela. Can you tell us about yourself, your company, and what are your roles and responsibilities?

Daniela: I work for a women's specialty retailer's digital division. My team is responsible for reporting out on digital performance and supporting cross-functional partners in category analysis, testing, and other key objectives.

Interviewer: Have you had the same role since you joined? And how did COVID affect the working and professional environment at the company? Have you been to the office yet by any chance?

Daniela: Yes, I have had the same role since I joined in June 2021. While my team is on a hybrid model, I have been into the office several times.

Interviewer: Perhaps that is one aspect of their approach to digital transformation. From what your experience, how would you interpret the term?

Daniela: As an undergraduate, I associated the word 'digital' and 'analytics' to heavy coding/data science. Regardless of the coding platform, that wasn't my area of interest. While I developed coding abilities through my undergraduate, graduate and professional experiences, my interpretation of the term has changed. Now, I think of digital analytics as a separate entity to data science or IT that is focused on storytelling and developing actionable insights.

Interviewer: So you code much less than you used to. Do you spend more time supervising the results and interpreting what has to be done next?

Daniela: In my role now, I spend time supervising/interpreting the results and sharing out those results to key stakeholders. I started my career in market research and was very involved in coding raw data to enable it to be transformed and read. While I found it rewarding, I was more interested in working in-house where these insights would be used to make actionable decisions.

Interviewer: What is your current position at the women's specialty retailer? Do your clients come to you with requests within the firm, like having internal clients?

Daniela: I'm the senior analyst for the enterprise analytics team. Some of my "clients" include the digital merchandising team. I work cross-functionally with colleagues in project management, category management and finance to provide them with the data and insights necessary to make business decisions.

Interviewer: In terms of getting things done and making it more digital, what kinds of efforts seem to work well in getting people on board to do A/B testing or to do things that are more around digital transformation, and what things don't work well?

Daniela: I think it depends on the question being asked, the level of data that is available, and cross-functional bandwidth, and most importantly, the alignment of the question with the business's key objectives. For me, relevant questions would include what the test objective is, what data already exists, what is feasible from a set up/ platform perspective, and what the level-of-effort to get a test off the ground is. To receive cross-functional buy-in, all team members need to be aligned on objectives. Without internal alignment or mutual understanding of the goal, tests and other projects will not move forward or work less effectively. At the end of the day, our mutual goal is to improve the customer experience in a way that makes sense and does not jeopardize the business or integrity of the data.

Interviewer: When you talk about these skills, are you thinking about conducting analyses in a way that show you actionable insights? Is there an obvious emphasis on online versus retail sales in terms of importance?

Daniela: Yes, and infrastructure plays a huge role in conducting any sort of analysis. My company has developed the infrastructure that enables data users to access data and manipulate the data to answer business questions. This women's specialty retailer views digital and store sales as equally important, with the digital business being the "largest" store that needs to be merchandised and branded consistently. In my experience, I've realized not all companies have the caliber of data my company does. In fact, to achieve such a high caliber would be costly as retroactively cleaning the data would propose its own challenges as data inputs and outputs may not have remained consistent or existed at all.

Interviewer: Do you see what makes a particularly effective either manager in this space or effective strategy in this space compared to others? Like hiring or communicating the vision or supporting training and other kinds of qualities that you feel makes a team more capable?

Daniela: In my opinion, what makes an effective manager in this space is like what makes an effective manager in other spaces. The difference is understanding the goals and creating the strategy to get there and flexing that strategy as needed based on the business objectives. I think it is important to not only have a holistic view of the business, but also to create a team that has both the hard and soft skills to achieve short- and long-term goals.

Interviewer: Thank you so much for your time and for providing insights. I think we couldn't get these thoughts from other perspectives because you're right in the middle of this journey as individual, but also as companies are going through the journey.

Daniela: In the last 7–8 years, digital analytics has exploded and become increasingly important to organizations, which is to your point around the time I graduated and was starting to pivot my career to digital analytics. We know that all-things digital is driving the world. The questions now are how organizations should collect and organize data, and how that data should be applied to its output. It's critical for businesses to evolve their processes to keep-up with customer expectations and behavior.

NEIL HOYNE

Chief Measurement Strategist

Interviewer: Thanks for joining us for a speed chat about digital transformation Neil.

Neil: My pleasure. I recently published a book called *Converted* that looks at the power of data to help organizations understand customers and it's an exciting area to be exploring and helping people.

Interviewer: In your view, what has been the reason for many less-than-stellar digital transformations in companies?

Neil: Digital transformation was straightforward early on. The focus was making manual processes digital. For example, transitioning from fax forms to online forms. This process later became generalized as digital transformation. The connection to the root processes was lost. Digital transformation became a goal in itself rather than a link to improving an underlying task/action. This resulted in broad efforts to bring in the cloud, SQL, etc., but without asking "why" or "how" enough in relation to these efforts.

Interviewer: What ways does this overly broad approach manifest in organizations?

Neil: One way this appears is the celebration of mediocre transformations, often because the budget expenditure was so large that it became difficult not to accept a result as anything less than successful. For example, a capability such as curbside pickup was celebrated, yet for many customers the value was marginal at best. This didn't stop many companies pursuing curbside pickup as a new approach as competitors were often racing to enable this service, without first examining the actual value to the customer. Following the herd in DT has replaced understanding core processes and why these processes may need to be replaced or improved.

Interviewer: The worry of being left behind can indeed place pressure on decision makers. How can they ensure their efforts have real impact?

Neil: If you want to be truly successful at DT, forget the hype and get down to the core by asking: "What is it?." DT sounds great, but it must be clear that what are you actually doing is creating value. Often decision makers look to other companies to fill in the gaps. This can result in measures such as using a software to fill in perceived weaknesses when in fact the need is to analyze obsolete processes and leverage the opportunities and experiences for digital.

Interviewer: What hands-on approaches have you seen work during transformation efforts?

Neil: Pick something small you want to make digital. For example, curbside pickup. Identify what made it work, repeat for the next process and again identify what made it work. Keep improving, keep deploying. Start small, understand, then extend. Companies learn a lot more this way.

Interviewer: Thank you for sharing actionable insight in such a short chat. It's stimulating to here how companies are facing these challenges with actionable measures.

Neil: There are many successful digital transformations and each one we can help is a success in itself!

MEREDITH MACHOVOE

Head of Business Insights

Interviewer: Thanks Meredith for joining us! To kick this off, could you tell us a little bit about what you do in your day-to-day responsibilities and anything that might be related to digital transformation?

Meredith: I'm the Head of Business at a Workflow software company. I lead a team called Research and Insights and the insights side is what we do, the research side is more aspirational. We're using a lot of internal data to try to understand what's going on in the business. We have three main deliverables inside studies: those are typically, five-to-eight week deep dives that could use multivariate regression techniques to determine how much it matters, what are the key levers, what should the business do, etc.? The second deliverable is top-down machine learning models which are kind of more financial models, trying to project where we will land this quarter, the next three quarters after that. What will happen to our gross retention, our net retention? How much pipeline coverage do we need? The third component of what we deliver is around proactive insights. So, looking across our knowledge graph for our set of interconnected dashboards, looking at what's happening in the business, what's happening internally and externally, can we proactively alert our stakeholders as to what might happen? That includes monitoring our predictions and trying to understand why they change. I work across the company; partner a lot with the corporate strategy team, our Finance Planning and Analytics team, Ops functions as well as key business units throughout the company. We do studies that are both external; meaning about our customers, products and services and as well as internal about our employees' retention and employee voice surveys.

Interviewer: Is that a structure where your clients are internal to the firm, they're all coming to you for help, and advice and expertise?

Meredith: I'm not customer facing but I'm internal stakeholder facing. My longer-term studies are VP + sponsored with a committed action. So, we don't go in unless you say, "Hey, this is a decision I'm trying to make, you put your name on it and say this is what I'm actually going to do with this data," then we'll prioritize it. I run a steerco (a steering committee) and an operating committee. The steerco helps with prioritization and to ensure I'm working on the most important questions for the company. They give guidance as to what things seem to matter most and what decisions we should make going forward.

Interviewer: How would you describe your workflow software company?

Meredith: I would say the thing that is great about the company is that we were born online. We were born on the cloud. A lot of the older tech companies were born in a different world where things were manual. There's a lot of tech debt, a lot of code monoliths that they haven't been able to transform. From a data and analytics perspective, it makes life a whole lot easier because the data are naturally more interconnected because it was born online. The field of data and analytics grows so quickly.

Interviewer: This is fascinating. It's also good to hear your perspective for the future questions as well, comparing the earlier experiences you had with what you have from a digitally born company.

Meredith: I started my career in banking, where we were still using mainframes and that was early on, 2004–2005, prefinancial crisis. We were joking that we almost had to take the holes off the side of the paper at that point, but I think things have really grown and changed; but coming back to the company, our business is digital transformation and so if we aren't drinking our own champagne, eating our own dog food, it would be hard to then go tell the world that they need to be digitally transformed. All of our products and services are really around that idea of how we transform the world, how do we transform every company, how do we make the world work better for everyone, how do we connect things across all the disparate systems through our platform. From an analytics perspective, how do we become that digital brain for the company?

Interviewer: From a very broad perspective on how digital transformation is accepted or not accepted across companies of many types, can you speak a little bit about companies that natively seem to adopt it more smoothly versus those that seem to find a little bit more challenging?

Meredith: Analytics was first becoming a thing when I joined in the banking sector, and that was really the only industry kind of really leaning into analytics at that time. But again, the data were all over the place. Someone manually tracks it in this spreadsheet over here, and you're challenged to automate and get it into the right place. There's a lot of roadblocks, and that's where I say there's a lot of tech debt and to go out to the mainframe and figure out how to get it out of something, and a lot of work being done just to get to the data to make the right decision. My first company in Tech was a financial services software company and it was fascinating because I had to jump through hoops just to get direct access to the data and take SQL tests (for access). I was there for almost nine years so things changed and grew. I work at a place now where there are less hoops to jump through. When we think of new products and new tools, we think integration first and API first and to get the right data in. I feel like it's much easier in a digitally born company and a cloud born company.

Interviewer: Even in this cloud born digitally born firm, what kind of impediments might still exist?

Meredith: I think on the business side, they're naturally skeptical. I'd say throughout my career I've seen, how data driven a company is. There are companies who say they're data driven, but they just use data to confirm the decision they've already made, and it can be frustrating. On the business side, because there's so much expertise, especially at those higher levels, there's a natural skepticism. Anyone needs to explain the model's ability. Our models are built top down. We took certain design decisions to make them more explainable. We could have built a more accurate model, but the purpose was not to have a black box. The purpose was to make it so any leader could understand it and then build the credibility and trust so they start to use it.

Interviewer: Are there typical tools or approaches that seem to make some machine learning methods more explainable or consistently useful?

Meredith: In my team, what we do at the heart of it is add the business context. It can't just be about the math. It must be about the business, how do I interpret it, putting myself in the shoes of the stakeholder. What data do I need to make that decision and what am I looking at daily? That's going to tell me more about the work. When we launched our newest model, we usually share things in a PowerPoint deck which it not full model documentation, but it allows you to have multiple visualizations. We have the visual representation version, the high level detailed version and then the spreadsheet math version. I did my masters in math, so I'm very familiar with this and I was looking at secondary education for a while, and I was tutoring math. A lot of people are afraid of math: they just hear numbers, and block it out, and can't look at it anymore. In analytics, that's the challenge, it's 95% accurate and it's going to give you numbers, but we need to help people learn how to interpret them.

Interviewer: What would be in a wish list to make your job easier in terms of encouraging digital transformation, make results more digestible, anything at all?

Meredith: Personally, I love my job, it's my dream job and I tell people that all the time. It is being able to guide the business with the mixture of the context as well as bringing the data, and our job is to make it approachable. Our job is to explain it in such a way that is easy to make the decision. Insights without action are completely meaningless, one can have the most amazing model, the most incredible insight, but if nobody uses it, then it's failure. A lot of people just put dashboards out, and say "here's the data." However, we really need to focus on usability, UI, UX and learning styles. Because not everybody can just stare at a dashboard and read those charts. Picture this, someone sent you a dashboard, you open it, and you can't even look it ... even though you like math. Increasingly, as more firms go to this digital transformation space where all the data are there, we need to make sure that we're still paying attention to *how people learn and understand, see and visualize data because it's not one size that fits all.*

Interviewer: Do you or your group or Human Resources, do anything to train your stakeholders to absorb data a little better?

Meredith: We do have a full training and support team. We do executive onboarding, take them through the critical dashboards for their space also, take them through our customer journey map and show them where all our studies are. There are enablement sessions that come out from there where we'll sit and help people understand how to use the dashboard and so forth, and they'll take feedback and iterate on it. All our dashboards have product managers who are managing that as a product, working to make sure that it is being used, it has good usability, and answering the questions that we set out to answer. This is the first data and analytics organization that I've been a part of that has UI/UX designers who advise on design principles. There's also business context visualization and that's where my team is also helping to consult in across the rest of our vertical teams and across the dashboards. If you're asking the user to complete multiple steps and do multiple calculations to figure out trends – is it good or bad – that's also a problem. I think about how digital transformation must go. It had to go from all these disparate systems, now it's all online, now it talks to each other. Users understand it and can just go and make decisions. That's where we need to get to, and I'd say we're on the journey, but we're not there yet.

Interviewer: It sounds like that's some of the secret sauce in the UX and business contexts?

Meredith: Absolutely. Whenever I say it's my dream job, it's because I've done many other parts of data and analytics: from the data warehouse, reporting, to data science models. But my sweet spot is right here where I get to take the business context, do the study, and guide the business. It frustrates me when I can't get to the information and trends I need from dashboards easily.

Interviewer: You mentioned the journey that the companies are taking, that's pretty much what we are trying to map out and perhaps highlight some of the end stage issues.

Meredith: Yes, and I think the trends that you're going to start seeing include Citizen AI developers and citizens this and citizen that, which is helpful. But again, if you aren't making the data explainable in context and you don't make it easy, that's going to be a disaster. With ML, I think the trend we're seeing is the human-in-the-loop is the way to help gain buy-in from the business side and stakeholders. With the human-in-the-loop, the model spits something out and the recipient can give us feedback. We can incorporate that back into the model and that helps the business stakeholders get more trust in the model. It feels less of a black box.

Interviewer: We're toying with the title of developing data democratization, making it easier for people to understand and use the data so they can be a part of the processes. Your experience fits nicely.

Meredith: Awesome, that's great to hear. I'm glad this was useful.

DAVID SAFFO

Researcher and Doctoral Candidate in Computer Science

Interviewer: David, you have seen digital transformation up close as a computer scientist. Can you please describe your day-to-day position or role and how it relates to digital transformation?

David: I work in the visualization lab, so we do data visualization and human computer interaction research. Data visualization takes raw data and studies all the different novel encodings like visual abstractions that are more easily digestible by humans. The field has been picking up steam for the past 10 years. It's right in line with statisticians and business analysts but is exploding into every domain where people have raw data and need a way to digest it more easily. We come in and do studies on the different visual encodings that we can use to make this interdisciplinary data, multimodal data more digestive. This can be done in many ways; like graphical perception studies, showing results on a bar graph or pie chart where it is simpler for humans to perceive position versus area. There are more interdisciplinary works like domain studies and design studies, which is when you work with a domain collaborator to figure out their tasks and their needs and transform those tasks into data abstractions that you can implement tools with. I did one personally for visualizing drone data.

Interviewer: Can you tell us more about the drone data visualization work?

David: Sure, we start from open-source flight software that collects logs from all these drones. These drones that have different sensors, and I did a design study where I worked with this community to develop an online tool. Basically, it aims to combine all the sensor data with the geographical position of the drone at the time and incorporating those two in time series and Geo position data.

The human computer interaction side of things is making sure all these tools are user friendly and easy to use; that's done by examining user behavior through controlled studies where you give users a set of tasks and you ask them to execute it and you can record the completion time and examine their behavior in speak aloud protocols and afterwards go through and do what we'd call open coding.

Interviewer: Do you think virtual reality is stepping in?

David: For me, it is now coming in. The virtual reality subdomain which we call immersive analytics, where the goal is to use emerging display technologies to do data visualization and analytical tasks. The most interesting part about it is, when you look at data visualization, it almost feels like we're getting to the point where we tried everything. There are so many shapes you can use to encode data before you see it on 2D. Adding the third dimension, the possibilities open way more and things are much less clear on how to design things for 3D space versus 2D space. 3D encodings that typically would be frowned upon by the visualization community – there's sort of unjustified 3D – 2D is usually always seen as better, but when you add VR in stereoscopic vision that changes a lot.

Interviewer: This is interesting because there's even a level of conservatism, in a field as innovative as your own; 2D versus 3D.

David: I agree, and you run into problems with reviewers where you'll submit a paper using VR and 3D encodings, and you'll get a reviewer who doesn't understand the immersive analytics realm. For them it is not acceptable, your paper is ignored. A lot of times they haven't tried virtual surrounding themselves. They don't know how much better it is, how better 3D is when you have your actual depth perception there.

Interviewer: What about barriers to adoption? Are other kinds of potential impediments to advancements in this that they come to mind. From a research side or from an industry side?

David: The industry side is kind of a barrier for adoption. In the research side where we do user studies, one of the critical problems is to recruit remote participants and experienced participants, because the adoption isn't there. You never have to teach someone how to use a mouse and keyboard. I don't have to explain it, but for a VR headset, if they haven't tried it before, I will have to explain it to them and you will see the difference in performance between an experienced VR user and inexperienced VR user, so that can complicate studies. The second part is we've gotten comfortable using mechanical turk and other crowdsourcing techniques to recruit huge amounts of diverse participants for traditional data visualization studies. There's a ton of research now coming out on how to remedy this. I have a paper on this subject which uses social VR platforms like VR Chat, which I talked about briefly in the 2021 DATA Forum panel. You can implement custom worlds with custom scripts, so why not do so to experiment on user performance? One must get creative with how to extract data. We took screenshots of data printed on a wall and then used optimal character recognition to convert it, like video recordings and examine behavior that way.

Interviewer: Talking about hardware versus software; you being inclined more toward software, is that a barrier? VR headsets are not universal. What's slowing the software down?

David: The bottleneck is probably the hardware, but that's not an excuse for the software being as far behind as it is. One of my favorite Twitter posts was like "VR is in the Geocity Era, and everything is going to look very cringy and tacky." We don't quite understand how to do UI, fluid interactions and how to represent ourselves in VR. It's the user and the lack of adoption slowing down the process.

Web VR particularly is far behind when you compare the number of frameworks and resources available for programming things on the web-to-web VR. I didn't realize how spoiled I was with how easy it is to make things for the web on desktop and then switching over to Web VR. You basically must build everything from scratch, as things don't really exist like libraries to help you. Except for the core structure, everything else you have to do on your own.

Interviewer: Where is the strong drive for change going to come from?

David: AR certainly is getting huge push from the DoD and also from manufacturing. The defense industry and medicine are the biggest industry drivers right now. Different applications like that are being able to display schematics while they're working on the assembly line for AR and then VR for training use to get a more immersive experience while training on how to assemble these pieces. In both defense and medicine, there's a lot of training for AR and VR. These are the biggest industry pushers. The biggest push is going to be consumers and whatever Oculus continues to do, as they're heavily subsidizing their devices. Valve has slowed down, even though its Index VR is on the top seller list on Steam again. Their issues are price and convenience: the Index costs $1,000 and has wires coming out everywhere. So, for general consumers, I think the biggest barrier is reducing the friction and putting on the headset and just making it as convenient as possible. You know the Quest; it runs just fine and has streaming capabilities.

Interviewer: How are people adapting to expensive hardware development or is it just a matter of bringing the whole cost down?

David: Yes, it's bringing the whole cost down but not too much, one because Quest is cheap and Facebook is probably subsidizing it too much. This could negatively affect the industry because not everyone is going to be able to subsidize. At the end of the day, there's a lot of Quest experiences that are too arcade-y, and it feels more like a mobile, like early mobile gaming than it does like a proper VR experience. That can turn a lot of people off. I don't want things to get too inexpensive because you still need to push the capable hardware abilities and the display technology especially when we can be the game changers to get better at manufacturing micro-LED displays and tiny headsets. Cutting cost is going to increase competition for other entrants trying to enter the market. The company Deca Gear are planning to make their own headset, they had a Kickstarter, but now there's a lot of doubts that they will survive. It is because they're trying to be price competitive with Facebook; they're manufacturing hip trackers; rumors say that it's not going well.

Interviewer: So who's the biggest player likely to challenge Quest and Facebook?

David: Everyone thinks it's Apple. They are hiring AR, VR people. Some of the rumors are hilarious such as they were going to sell one per day per store making it exclusive, which is technically and financially not acceptable. Someone else said this in another conversation, even for a book regarding electric cars. They said: "Oh, Apple," about the Apple car; they are working on it. Not sure whether it is going to be successful or not. Same thing for the VR headset. Apple has had products that flopped and everyone kind of forgets about that. They are effective at releasing technology that is often presented as new and getting everyone to believe this newness and become excited about it. I can see them being a huge catalyst for the industry.

Interviewer: Being in the research environment, do you have an opinion on how the innovations such as software or hardware from universities, are going to get out more effectively? Do you think a lot is going to come directly from the R&D groups within the companies, rather than universities?

David: I might be a little biased, but I think the internal R&D groups are hiring people from academia, from where the research starts. Then those people move into the industry positions with that experience and thus bring it to industry. A lot of academics are not interested in making their work translational as graduate students are not good software developers and they aren't given the time to. Otherwise they can't publish.

Interviewer: Who are the kinds of people that the companies are targeting? Graduate master students to PhD students, who spend much time in coding?

David: Hiring in the software realm is messed up right now with coding interviews. PhD candidates are at a disadvantage because master students spend all their time coding, and they also have a lot more time to be studying for interviews and will be able to answer how to flip a tree. These internal R&D companies tend to hire at conferences and interview PhD students for role of software engineers. The PhD might get you the interview, but it's not going to help you with the HR person on the end or technical part, where the master's student has an edge.

Interviewer: What do computer science professors expect of their doctoral students when they graduate? Are they grooming all to be professors or are they happy with big companies hiring their students?

David: That depends on the professor, I've heard horror stories of like "never mention to professor that you want to go to industry; they'll ignore you for the rest of your PhD," some are adamant on only training, others are open to whatever you want to do. My advisor is very supportive of whatever I want to pursue and will help me that way. Talking about myself, I applied straight out of undergraduate, and didn't know what data visualization was as a research discipline. It worked out for me but giving advice to a younger student? For that you need a supportive advisor.

Interviewer: So anything that you'd like to add before we finish? Regarding insights into how things are going to change in the future?

David: I had one thing to add, the headline of my thesis is that the death of the desktop is not coming. It's been touted for long now. The desktop is not going to die, and VR is not going to replace it, but it is going to augment the desktop essentially, it's going to complement it like mobile phones and VR AR is going to be the same way.

TYLER SHANNON

Senior Design Strategist

Interviewer: Please describe your day-to-day job in nutshell

Tyler: I'm primarily in a consulting role right now, and have several clients that I work with. My day-to-day involves project management with a lot of client and consultant meetings. As projects progress through their delivery phases, I transition from project management and stakeholder research to actual analytics, data science, insight mining, driving recommendations for my clients. Right now, the two main projects that I am supporting are in early research and scoping phases: a lot of meetings, stakeholder engagement and business case analysis.

Interviewer: This sounds like an MBA-like experience.

Tyler: I don't have any formal training that is comparable to an MBA, but a lot of the work I do with my clients is focused on putting data to use to help their organizations meet the business goals. In the past couple of years, we have seen COVID impact the rate at which companies are adopting digital. Our staff was in person in office, and we had overnight transition to a remote work environment and so our need for digital transformation has increased quite rapidly and we're seeing similar needs from our clients. Four years ago, in November 2017, I was brought onto the team to help build out a data science practice and since then, we've been developing that capability. For a long time, I've been working directly with the partners of our firm to identify what it means to have a data scientist in an architecture firm and planning firm. The industry and our services use data science and informed decision-making techniques. A lot of our clients push for state of art solutions that are senior leadership level driven.

Interviewer: Your experience and time at General Assembly was not related to any position, it kind of happened.

Tyler: I went into General Assembly with an open mind about where it would take my career. I didn't have full intentions of applying it to the industry that I was in already, but it happened. When you're working in data science, it helps to have a good understanding of the domain that you're working in so, you can understand how your modeling techniques get applied. Ten years of experience working in professional architecture environments made sense. I apply what I learned in General Assembly to this industry.

Interviewer: It sounds like in hindsight you're custom made for the job, in some respects it is your profile. I'm assuming it's unusual for someone of your profile to be in this position.

Tyler: It's not a common role, so most architecture firms don't have in-house data scientists on staff, but I think that is going to change. I think that more and more firms are looking to a role like mine to bring in house, but most firms don't have someone on staff, so the role is very much unique and that's differentiator for us. The clients that we're working with now are looking for data-driven solutions to the challenges that they are facing in their businesses. We're able to leverage skill set working with data to drive some pretty unique solutions for them.

Interviewer: Scene leadership was looking for ways to make better informed, data-driven decisions, or at least informed decisions. How we're doing better data is one of the ways, and it's still a rare role for an architectural firm. Has this meant that clients that typically would have served anyway are being served at a higher level? Or is it also opening a new world of clients that wouldn't otherwise be addressable?

Tyler: Yes, I think it's a little bit of both. The suite of base services that we offer to clients, is now being supplemented by my work. And there are entirely new types of contracts that we're able to service with my expertise in-house. The first major contract that we signed was new for us, after I came on board was for a university in the Greater Boston area to understand the impacts of infrastructure, investments that they were planning on making. We conducted an impact report for them that analyzed their existing conditions and did some scenario modeling on what they could expect in terms of business impacts.

Interviewer: Is there any challenge in representing an architecture firm as data-centric people may not quite understand what that means?

Tyler: The first couple of years of me being on board, there were lots of change in conversations around how our firm is viewed in the industry's eyes. This is the 60th year of this firm. Before I came on board the firm did traditional architecture planning, interior design work and that was how people, and our clients knew us in the industry. The first few years were about changing the perception, supplementing our client base and industry's knowledge of what we do as a company. There were many meeting and important calls with clients to prove them this is what our design looks like, our worth and changes that would uplift your business. You should be thinking about data as a driver of your decisions.

Interviewer: Is it naturally permeating architecture firms and so every firm over a certain scale is going to have this function, and, should the education and architects be changing universities to more naturally incorporate this?

Tyler: To answer your first question, I don't think that it's going to be a rapid change. I think architects are creatures of habit. It takes a lot to change the behavior of an office, work culture; takes time, takes patience. I don't think that architecture firms are going to rapidly adopt data science or hire data scientists quickly, but the way architects and clients make decisions are changing. There will be an increasing need for dedicated data scientists. For the second question, I think that architecture education absolutely has to change. I think that architecture education must broaden its perspective a bit, it needs to be more interdisciplinary. Northeastern is doing this where they offer their architecture students the opportunity to go take classes in other fields. It's important for students to get a broader perspective, supplemented by the design thinking.

Interviewer: Is design thinking a standard part of most architecture degrees these days?

Tyler: I think people approach it differently, schools have different opinions. I went to Northeastern for two years and then I transferred to NC State in Raleigh. Northeastern didn't have a very specific design thinking curriculum, it was sort of embedded in all these other classes that students would take at NC State.

Interviewer: I was a certified design thinker from IDEO back in 2015. But even in the business school, part of the challenge was trying to tell people what design thinking is good for. Maybe it is because it's too close for comfort. In business contexts it is quite fascinating to see how it affects things like the clients might be the drive to adapt and change. Of course education might lead or lag depending upon the institution. Clients know that they need to be using their digital assets, their data assets differently, and in a more informed way. They have a bunch of data and it's not necessarily in any organized database or warehouse.

Tyler: Clients are currently trying to figure out how to better leverage their data assets, and define what types of challenges their business is facing. And I think it's iterative. We're not going to solve all their digital challenges in one day. Consultants anticipate the need of the clients that is iterative. It is an agile approach where proposing, trying, learning more about the objective makes sense, then sort of making pivots and adjusting business needs. Flexibility and sensitivity to that is important.

Interviewer: In a company we talk a lot about roles where issues are discussed, and it becomes therapy. What are we supposed to do when we want to hire a person? If you want to be more involved with Northeastern or in general so the forum you know is an annual event? But in terms of networking of having industry people connect we are in a critical position to create these events in the past.

Tyler: The conversations, and the data forum were both valuable concepts. I'd love to stay involved in any way that makes sense. Just stay in touch, if there's an event coming up and I'd love to hear about it!

NOTES

1. Some of the company names have been redacted by request.
2. https://www.science.org/doi/abs/10.1126/science.aax2342

INDEX

Printed in the United States
by Baker & Taylor Publisher Services